INSIDE VOICES OUTSIDE LIGHT

SIGURÐUR PÁLSSON

INSIDE VOICES OUTSIDE LIGHT

Translated & introduced by

Martin S. Regal

ARC
PUBLICATIONS
2014

Published by Arc Publications,
Nanholme Mill, Shaw Wood Road
Todmorden OL14 6DA, UK

Original poems copyright © Sigurður Pálsson 2014
Translation copyright © Martin S. Regal 2014
Introduction copyright © Martin S. Regal 2014
Copyright in the present edition © Arc Publications 2014

978 1906570 58 3 (pbk)
978 1906570 59 0 (hbk)

Design by Tony Ward
Printed in Great Britain by
TJ International, Padstow, Cornwall

ACKNOWLEDGEMENTS
The present volume contains poems selected from
eleven of the fifteen books of Sigurður Palsson's poetry
that were published between 1980 and 2012.

Cover photograph by Páll Stefánsson

This book has been translated with a financial support of

MIÐSTÖÐ ÍSLENSKRA BÓKMENNTA
ICELANDIC LITERATURE CENTER

Supported using public funding by
ARTS COUNCIL
ENGLAND
LOTTERY FUNDED

'Arc Translations'
Series Editor: Jean Boase-Beier

CONTENTS

Jón Yngvi Jóhannsson: Were you constantly composing
   when you were a child, Sigurður?
Sigurður Pálsson: No, I didn't *compose* a thing. On the other
   hand, I was always *writing*.[1]

The above is taken from a public interview with Sigurður
Pálsson. In his typically humble fashion, but spiced with a
dash of humour, Pálsson tells his audience that as a child he
had thoughts of becoming a goldsmith, a painter and a writer
– clearly distinguishing the verb *að skrifa* [to write] from *að
yrkja* [to compose], the latter of which is only used for compos-
ing poetry. As it turned out, he opted for the last, becoming
a writer in the broadest sense of the word, winning numer-
ous nominations and awards for poems, his prose works,
his plays and his translations, both in Iceland and in France.
However, he is not very well known in the English-speaking
world. This book hopes to go some way towards redressing
that imbalance and thereby give much greater access to his
poetry than has hitherto been possible. That is its primary
aim.

Hopefully, the idea that any poetry worth the name re-
quires no contextualization died out with New Criticism, that
brand of literary "analysis" that notoriously ignored time,
place and circumstance in an attempt to place literary studies
on a more scientific basis. The truth is that while good litera-
ture, and especially good poetry, tends to rise above its imme-
diate cultural context and (translators dare to hope) above its
source language, some basic explanation can help accelerate
the process. Aside from my glancing treatment of the poem
'Plywood' (p. 65), a little later on in this introduction, there is
no attempt here to explicate the poems themselves, or indeed
even to justify why I chose one English word or phrase over
another – that is left entirely to the reader. However, I feel that

---

[1] "Varstu síyrkjandi í barnæsku Sigurður?" "Nei, ég orti ekki neitt. Hins
vegar var ég alltaf skrifandi." *Sigurður Pálsson: Ritþing,* 28 April 2001:
Menningarmiðstöðin Gerðuberg, p. 5.

Pálsson's poems do require some kind of contextualization, regarding both the milieu out of which they emerged and, just as importantly, their overall structure as perceived by the poet in the process of writing.

Arc Publications recently brought out *Bloodhoof*, a single volume of poems by the Icelandic writer Gerður Kristný Guðjónsdóttir, a narrative sequence inspired by the *Poetic Edda*. Both the volume itself and the English translation are considerable achievements, and not least because Gerður Kristný is not only a poet but also the author of a number of best-selling novels for young readers, a writer of short stories and novels for adults and, most recently, an adapter of her own work to the musical stage. I expect she would also describe herself as a *writer* with similar humility. Justifiably proud of (and still influenced by) ancient traditions, Icelanders regard themselves not only inheritors of the land of the sagas and of Eddic poetry, but also as a highly technologically advanced and ultra modern society, in which book and computer literacy are amongst the highest in the world. It still surprises me that the best sales' period for books is Christmas. This is because Icelanders have a long tradition of buying each other books as Christmas gifts. Icelanders are avid readers, both through those long, dark winter nights and those endless summer days. As representatives of the tourist industry never tire of reminding us, Iceland is a country of striking contrasts. Geologically speaking, it is a relatively new land mass, having been pushed up out of the sea during the Miocene Period some twenty million years ago. As a direct result of its comparatively late appearance, very little fauna evolved on the island aside from birds. Indeed, its only indigenous land mammal is the arctic fox, which is believed to have walked to it across the frozen wastes of the north at the end of the last Ice Age. All other mammals – mice, rats, cats, dogs and livestock, even reindeer – were introduced by man. Its range of flora is similarly limited, though more varied than one might imagine. For most of its history, what is now called Iceland remained untouched by anything but the elements. Then, in the ninth century AD, and for reasons that no one has successfully explained, the first wave of settlers began to arrive – and everything changed.

Having made their way in boats (principally from Norway),

the first "Icelanders" faced no native population to negotiate with, overcome or displace. The only residents on the vast island were a scattering of Irish monks, known in Icelandic as *papar*, who lived here as hermits and therefore in isolation even from one another. Their number can only be guessed at. But whatever presence they may have had, it appears not to have had any measurable impact on later Icelandic culture. Like the Polynesians who first settled New Zealand, the Icelanders had that rare opportunity to form a new nation with its own natural boundaries. Indeed, they were in many ways more fortunate than their Maori counterparts because when their country was later colonized by a succession of foreign powers, their new masters were mostly content to rule and extract taxes from a distance and leave the natives very much to their own devices. In the few centuries after the settlement (874 AD), Icelanders enjoyed intermittent freedom from the machinations of various Norwegian kings and established an independent democracy. But it was short-lived. By the thirteenth century, that political independence was lost and it took them almost a millennium to reclaim it.

However, although much of the subject matter of ancient Norse poetry was common to all the people who spoke its variant dialects, only the Icelanders managed to develop a new form of literature, the sagas, and only the Icelanders managed to preserve a literary tradition that reached back across the centuries. Like so many other early democracies (Athens, Sparta, Republican Rome), Iceland was governed by chieftains and readily availed itself of slaves, many of whom were Celts, both from Ireland and what are now called the British Isles. Indeed, it has often been suggested that the substantial literary achievements of the Icelanders derived from the Celtic elements of their culture. Certainly, the fact that no comparable store of literary treasures can be found among the other Nordic nations during the early medieval period, has led to the conjecture that they inherited more from the Celts than is usually acknowledged. Whatever the explanation for the appearance of the Icelandic sagas, they have served both to inspire later generations of poets and writers and, miraculously, to help preserve the Icelandic tongue to the extent that all Icelanders can still negotiate their way through those sagas successfully without any special knowledge or tuition. I use the word "miraculously" advisedly because Icelandic has survived through hundreds of years of Danish rule and nearly a century of English.

This is not intended as a potted history of Iceland or of the hardships Icelanders have had to endure over the twelve centuries that have passed since the first settlers arrived there. Rather, it is an attempt to provide a context for this particular writer. Located at what Icelanders sometimes call *á hjara veraldar* or "at the edge of the world", they are acutely aware of the precariousness of their existence in a place where the European and the American continents meet. They see themselves as Europeans but know that being so far from the European mainland substantially qualifies their European identity. The result is often a strange blend of protective insularity and an obsessive need for recognition by the outside world. For example, calling the country an island is virtually a taboo, doubly ironic since the Icelandic word for the country is Ísland. Like only a handful of other now modern societies, Iceland jumped from a predominantly agricultural to an advanced technological society without going through any of the intermediary stages. To this day, the only branch of economic activity that could be classified as anything like heavy industry is a couple of aluminium smelting plants. Massive rural depopulation over the past few decades has resulted not in people seeking employment in factories, but rather in various areas of commerce and trade. At the same time, Iceland has successfully managed to export its considerable expertise in geothermal and hydroelectric technology all over the globe. A good proportion of the population regard the unprecedented exploitation of the land and its natural resources as a catastrophe; the rest see it as both a desirable and inevitable stage in the country's belated industrialization.

Like many of his contemporaries, Pálsson straddles both worlds: an isolated agricultural society that has remained more or less unchanged for over a millennium and a twenty-first century virtual community. He is equally at home rounding up sheep and being a modern urban spectator, Walter Benjamin's perfect *flâneur*. Born on 30 July 1948, four years after Iceland snatched independence from a Denmark still embroiled in war and when the total population of the island was a mere 130,000, Pálsson was the child of ageing

11

parents. His father was fifty and his mother forty-three at the time of his birth. Advances in medicine had curbed what had been a staggeringly high infant mortality rate, but tuberculosis and hydatidosis were still common and diseases such as polio, an epidemic of which broke out in the north of Iceland in late 1948, were very difficult to contain. Pálsson says he succumbed so often to various illnesses in the first two years of his life that it became a cause of real concern to his family. In his biography, he wistfully reflects that he never got to know his father as well as his elder siblings but, typically for him, it also leads him into making what seems at first a rather strange numerical observation: namely, that he spans three centuries because his father was born in the nineteenth century and we are now in the twenty-first. As we shall see, numbers and mathematical calculation play a very important role in his life.

Sigurður Pálsson is both a typical and an atypical Icelander. Like most of his compatriots, he has a deep love of travelling and of absorbing and adapting all that he encounters on his travels. At the same time, he is one of the few major Icelandic writers who has looked repeatedly to France rather than to Scandinavia, Germany, or the English-speaking countries for his literary models. Iceland and France are, of course, long-standing allies, both priding themselves on being republics rather than kingdoms, and with evidence of a good deal of mixed blood, especially in the West Fjords. However, with the exception of the illustrious former president, Vigdís Finnabogadóttir (who, incidentally, was one of the people who taught Sigurður French) Iceland's cultural links with France have mainly been forged by a long line of tenacious individuals at the Icelandic branch of Alliances Françaises. Even the best known living Icelandic artist, Erró, almost regarded as half-French by Icelanders at least, was educated in Norway and Italy before taking up residence in Paris. In contrast, Sigurður's own relationship with France and French culture began when he was nineteen. Armed, by his own admission, with little more than grammar-school French and a head full of dreams and ambitions, he set out on a path that very few of his compatriots had trodden and travelled alone to Paris to embark on no less a task than studying for a degree in theatre studies at the Sorbonne. That was the beginning of a life-long adventure that eventually saw him being made a Chevalier de l'Ordre des Arts et Lettres in 1990 and Chevalier de l'Ordre du Mérite in 2007 by the President of France at the time, Jacques Chirac.

Pálsson reports his move to France while he was still in his teens with great skill and humour in *Minnisbók*, the first volume of his autobiography.[2] It opens with an account of how he arrived in Paris at nineteen years of age but "looking fourteen" and without any knowledge of the city he was to make his home for many years. Guided more by instinct than anything else, he hails a cab and asks the driver to take him to Boulevard Montparnasse, an area in which he assumed he might find suitable accommodation. When the taxi driver asks which number Boulevard Montparnasse he wants to go to, a simple enough question (although one that he had clearly not anticipated), Pálsson uses the opportunity to elaborate on why he chose the number 97:

> Suddenly, French numerals began to unfold in my mind's eye [as did] my French teachers, Vigdís Finnbogadóttir and Magnús G. Jónsson; I remembered how well Vigdís had taught us to rehearse those absurd combinations of numerals from ninety-seven to ninety-nine, *quatre-vingt-dix-sept*, comprising *four, twenty, ten, seven* and so on, and Vigdís smiled, and it was all so wonderful and shot through my mind in a flash, and I just rolled out: *Quatre-vingt-dix-sept*, ninety seven. (p. 10)

In the later volume, *Bernskubók*, which begins with his childhood, he similarly brings a certain kind of reckoning into play. Pálsson recalls early in this account that his first "writing project" was not an ode to nature or reflections on solitude but a precisely composed annal of haymaking in the summer of 1961, apparently one of the wettest anyone in the area could remember:

---

[2] *Minnisbók* (JVP Publishers: Reykjavík, 2007). The title of the first volume is better translated as "memoranda" than "memoirs", although the addition of *bók* (book) also suggests a notepad in which one jots down ideas. The epigraph at the front of the book is from Milan Kundera and translates as "Forgetfulness which obliterates and memory which transforms". However, since it remains untranslated I have chosen to refer to it as *Notebook* here.

At the end of the summer, this was in effect the outcome: disastrous haymaking, disastrous *Haymaking Annal.* Nevertheless, I had succeeded in completing that annal and even though it was not quite as brilliant as I had intended it to be when its perfect form first flashed in my mind, it was lying there before me like a sign.
Reality had constantly hindered the actual recording of reality and thereby disturbed it.
A vicious circle. I saw that at the end of that summer when I was thirteen. I had no idea at the time that this was my initiation as a writer. (p. 211)

So many important moments in Pálsson's life appear to have been marked either by the act of counting or by some association with numerals. Even the joke he makes about his father's diary entry the day he was born (which comprises an observation about the weather, and almost as an afterthought, the birth of his son), is tempered somewhat by Pálsson's own reflections on the fact that the temperature that day had risen to a record 30° Celsius. Icelandic readers are more likely to be surprised by this than foreigners. After all, the average temperature in Iceland for late July and early August is somewhere between 12-16° Celsius. We might be forgiven for thinking that Pálsson draws our attention to the fact that the temperature having risen to twice that figure made the event of his birth ominous in some way, but that is simply not true. Facts and figures, and particularly the latter, are very important to Pálsson as a writer. Two of his three novels take the names of geometrical objects: *Parísarhjól* [Ferris Wheel], (1998) and *Blár Þríhyrningur* [Blue Triangle], (2000), and one can find enumeration everywhere in his works, from seemingly incidental comments on his childhood to his appreciation of deeper patterns. For example, he reports in a diary entry made on 1 May 1957 (when he was 9) that he discovered "to [his] great astonishment that he recognized 82 of the 111 sheep". A subsequent entry, two weeks later, records that by then he knew them all by name, and Pálsson then produces the list as proof. Another thing with which he whiled away the time as a child was sitting on a grassy mound with a friend and writing down the names and number plates of passing cars. In both volumes, he invariably records the numbers of the houses or apartments at which he stayed or visited. Mentioning a little later in the book that his father owned a Willys Jeep, Pálsson clearly deems it perfectly natural to inform the reader not only of the jeep's registration number, but also of the age at which his father first learned to drive and the fact that he never exceeded a self-imposed speed limit of 40 kilometres per hour.

This preoccupation with numbers has also impacted the structure of Pálsson's poems, or rather their internal organization and the manner in which they have been collated into individual volumes. His first volume of poetry, *Ljóð vega salt*, appeared in 1975, and its title and structure were to provide a pattern for all his subsequent volumes. Every single one of the fifteen volumes of poetry that he has published to date bears a three-word title that begins with the word *ljóð*, a neuter word that serves as both the singular 'poem' and the plural 'poems' in Icelandic. Derived from the Old Norse *hljóð* (a contronym that still interestingly signifies both "sound" and "silence"), *ljóð* also stands at the centre of nearly one hundred compound words. Although Pálsson has said that he had no conscious intentions of arranging his work in such a manner at the outset, by the time he published his second volume of poetry, *Ljóð vega menn*, in 1980, a pattern had begun to emerge. From that time on, not only has each of his books of poetry begun with the word *ljóð*, they have been further divided into groups of three, where the second word remains the same and only the last changes. Thus his first book, *Ljóð vega salt* (1975) was followed by *Ljóð vega menn* (1980), and then by *Ljóð vega gerð* (1982). In the second series, *Ljóð námu land* (1985) was followed by *Ljóð námu menn* (1988) and then by *Ljóð námu völd* (1990). It may also be noted that each of these three words comprises four letters, a symmetry that may have led him to make a small modification by combining the three words of the title into one compound word from the third series onward. He has maintained this same pattern, his most recent volume bearing the title *Ljóðorkulind* (2012). Fascinatingly, though, instead of imposing strictures, this almost obsessive structuring allows Pálsson considerable freedom and gives rise to innumerable permutations of meaning that echo and resound throughout the books.[3]

---

[3] The contents list shows the simplest English versions of Pálsson's titles, the various significations of which are far too numerous to be recorded here.

For example, in the first of these "trilogies", *Ljóð vega salt*, the verb *að vega* variously means "to weigh", "to measure", "to balance", "to betray" or "to kill", while the noun *vegur* (*vega* being both its plural accusative and genitive form), means "road", "way" or "side". As an element in idiomatic phrases, *vega* becomes even more flexible. In one sense, too, Pálsson's permutations are about as close to being ideogrammatic as is possible while exclusively employing Latin graphemes. While *Ljóð vega salt* could be translated literally as "poem(s) measure(s) salt", the phrase *að vega salt* also means "to see-saw" or, by extension, "to be precariously balanced". At the same time, the middle voice form of the verb (*að vegast*) means "wandering around aimlessly". From the seventh volume onward (*Ljóðlínudans*, 1993) Pálsson's decision to amalgamate the three discrete words of each title in one longer word is partly typographical and partly a complex pun since the second and third word in the sequence usually form a compound word. Even non-Icelandic speakers will be able to see that the compound noun *línudans* means "line dance", and perhaps also that *ljóðlínu* means a line of poetry. Add to this the fact that the nominal form, *lína*, also has multiple significations of its own and you will begin to appreciate that Pálsson creates a veritable hoard of puns just within the titles of his books. In one sense, this organizing principle is artificial; it does not, for example, grow out of the poems themselves but is usually superimposed after the event – restructured rather than structured. Although Pálsson has always been interested in mathematics – he once described the New Mathematics of the 1960s to me as "magic" – and studied numerology for a period of time, he does not consider such activity as mystical, nor are his poems underpinned (or illuminated) by any belief that experience may be interpreted by numbers. Yet, at the same time, the numerical arrangement of his works is no more artificial than metre, measured in stresses and feet, or than rhyme that invests unlike words with a common sound. Indeed, most readers, Icelandic or otherwise, are hardly likely to take much notice of the internal numerical complexity of Pálsson's work because while it is undoubtedly pervasive, it remains largely unobtrusive. Icelandic critic Eiríkur Guðmundsson was the first to point out that the then recently published *Ljóðlínuskip* (1995), Pálsson's eighth volume of poetry, was divided into eight "chapters", the first of which comprised one poem, the second two, the third three, and so on through to eight.[4]

There are several reasons for drawing attention to this property of Pálsson's writing. Firstly, it goes some way to explain why it is unusually difficult to assemble a selection of his poems. In many cases, selecting anything but a whole series disturbs not only the internal balance but may also omit important points of reference. At the same time, there seems little justification for including all the poems in any given sequence solely on these grounds. Secondly, it alerts the reader to various guidelines or signposts, visible and audible, that help chart our way through his work. Thirdly, and most importantly, this structuring provides an insight into the ways in which Pálsson makes sense, or nonsense, of the world through the medium of words. Few Icelandic poets have a greater understanding of the intricacies of existential philosophy or a greater awareness of the absurd than Pálsson or, more significantly, of the balance between sense and nonsense. One of Pálsson's favourite metaphors for his style of writing is *flæði og farvegur* (literally "stream and riverbed"), but which signifies "fluidity and constraint", a method that can be applied equally to the poems themselves and the manner of their arrangement.

Guðmundsson also notes that Pálsson is one of the few poets of his generation to have kept faith with poetry. Most of his Icelandic contemporaries published a volume or two of poetry to begin with but then turned to the novel, for which they are best known today. Pálsson wrote novels and plays, in addition to various other works, but he is among the very few who has continued to publish volumes of poetry at regular intervals to the present day. When I asked him in an interview last year whether he was going to keep publishing them in threes, he responded with characteristic irony that it would be a catastrophe, of course, to die midway through a series – something he had to take into consideration now that he had "reached an age".[5] However, in another sense, Pálsson is completely

---

[4] 'Mörg andlit akasíutrésins'. *Skírnir* 170. Autumn, 1996, p. 478. The title of the article 'The Many Faces of the Acacia Tree' is borrowed from Pálsson's poem 'The Acacia Tree' (p. 69).
[5] Interview with the poet, July 2012. The transcript of this interview remains unpublished.

free of such restrictions. Not only has he experimented (very successfully) with other forms, he has also been highly unconventional in his poetry. Some of the poems are in tightly tuned metre; others are prose poems, and a third group pay no obvious attention to anything but to brevity and nuance. He sees the sentence as the unit of meaning in prose and the line as the unit of meaning in a poem. In most cases, there is a tension between the two that variously gives rise to either a precarious balance or a subtle iridescence.

Indeed, Pálsson's very method might be called prismatic, refractive rather than reflective. Guðbjörn Sigmundarson catches something of Pálsson's style when he says that it combines immediacy, an impressionistic view and enthusiasm.[6] Another characteristic is his ability to highlight an individual moment, and often by means of imperfect or asymmetrical repetition (if that is not a contradiction in terms). There are instances, too many to enumerate, where he appears (in prose and in poetry) to reiterate a point whereas he is in fact producing a slightly different version or angle or, in sonic terms, a kind of harmonic. He often talks about the combination of sound and sense in poetry but advises us not to ignore the visual dimensions of poetry, both in the patterning of the words in a line and the line on the page, but no less in the pictures or images that the words evoke. An attention to such detail may be traced to Pálsson's great admiration for Jacques Prévert. Undecided in the mid-1980s as to which of Prévert's poems he should translate, Pálsson ultimately elected to translate all of them. The influence from the avant-garde French poet is obvious in many places in Pálsson's own work, but perhaps most of all in his attention to minute detail and to exact rhythms. He has admitted more than once that Prévert's style was much more complex than he had ever imagined it to be. Pálsson also reminds us that Prévert was one of the most gifted screenplay writers of all time, numbering among his films *Les Enfants du*

---

[6] *Tímarit máls og menningar*, 1996, p. 135. Cited in Guðmundsson's article in *Skírnir* (see above note). "Sigurður Pálsson er skáld augnabliksins, skáld hrifningar og hughrifa [...]." "Augnabliksins" is a genitive meaning literally "of the moment", which suggests both a kind of transience and sense that the poet himself might soon become unfashionable. The latter is certainly not an obvious interpretation in the original.

Paradis, directed in 1945 by Marcel Carné – the film, incidentally, that Truffaut once said he would give up all his films to have directed. It was thus not only Prévert's exceptional talent for rendering the ordinary extraordinary, but an exact sense of visualisation that made him so outstanding.

Combining precision with a sense of humour and enthusiasm is no mean task and yet many people say that humour is the most difficult element to translate from one language to another. Humour, when not of the custard-pie or slipping on a banana skin variety, is usually topical. It requires a context. Thus, most satire not only fails to transcend language but is often limited to a specific period of time – one of the reasons that Jonathan Swift's vitriolic wit in *Gulliver's Travels* is often neutralised and regurgitated as a fairly harmless set of tales for children. However, Pálsson's humour is neither the pratfall kind, nor is it caustic. It derives instead from a sense of play. Occasionally, this takes the form of that well-known device, wordplay, but more often it is inherent in a situation or a process. 'A few practical exercises in event poetry', is an anachronistic piece that looks back to the 1960s, expressing the kind of sentiment one might find in a Roger McGough or Adrian Mitchell poem, although without the rhyme. The difference and a distinguishing mark of Pálsson's humour is the way in which he includes his volume of poems in the piece. In other words, this is no random "happening" but the actualisation of the very poem in which all the advice appears. This is not, admittedly, something that produces belly-laughter, but rather a sense of the absurd transformed into something palpable and tangible. The poem 'Beckett at the Closerie des Lilas' (p. 61), from the same volume, evinces a similar absurdity, where the poet recognises Samuel Beckett in a café, feels that he, the famous playwright and the waiter could all be in *Waiting for Godot*, but then realises that this "version" contains the wrong number of characters. Unable to decide whether he might be Lucky, Pozzo or Godot himself, the poet turns away from Beckett and ends the poem with an image of the afternoon edition of *Le Monde* coming "out of the green light". Like so many of Pálsson's humorous moments, this turns on something that did *not* take place, or an event that was displaced by another, usually of the most mundane kind but with a profound sensory effect – tactile, aural, visual or, in the case of the plywood 'map', olfactory.

I have translated the title of Pálsson's work *Minnisbók*, which traces his life from his childhood to his teens, as 'Memoranda', but it might equally be called *Hypomnemata* after the notebooks Plato advised his students to keep, and a term taken up later by Michel Foucault. Again, it is Guðmundsson who first alerts us to the correspondences between Foucault's ideas and Pálsson's practice, although he could not have known at the time that Pálsson would later adopt a term that paralleled *hypomnemata*.[7] However, the exact appellation is not the point. More importantly, it indicates that the events and objects scribbled down by the Greeks for future meditation and reflection were quite opposite to the semi-confessional notes recorded by monks to better understand the soul and the self. Even the most complex of Pálsson's images or meditations are outward looking, not products of a dramatized or analysed self; they are offerings to the reader rather than insights into the writer's mind. Icelandic, a language spoken by so few people and under enormous pressure for centuries, first from Danish and then from English, is nervously self-protective. Neologisms have to be endorsed by parliament and there is a movement that seeks to "purify" the language or at least curb its growing appropriation of English terms. Pálsson's position is clear on this matter. Language, he says, is not something that needs to be purified, it is something that operates out of a sense of discovery. While hardly an advocate of the new for its own sake, Pálsson has little interest in the opposite mode of preserving the archaic and the antique just because they are old.

English has traditionally been open to new coinages and nonce words, but while not exactly anathema to Icelandic, they are rare. Instead of creating new words, Pálsson is more likely to edge his way along a paradigmatic axis, placing adjectives alongside nouns that they would not usually modify. This is apparent in the earliest poems in this volume (which is chronologically arranged). However, literal translations of some of his images into English often sound even more surrealistic than they are. Thus, for example, "laughing, joined

[7] Guðmundsson, p. 484.

at the hip in an anorak" (in 'Nocturne for a Full Moon', p. 31) translates *hlæjandi samloka* (lit. "a laughing sandwich"). The Icelandic phrase *algjör samloka* ("an absolute sandwich") is commonly applied to two people who are inseparable. I therefore opted for "joined at the hip" instead of "sandwich" to describe the young couple, making their way across the square in the same anorak, 'domed' above their heads and thereby lose some of the playful punning of the original.. Similarly, I admit that the English "touched by the moon" does not capture the Icelandic *við tunglið*. In my version, the association is with lunacy while in the original it means "tipsy". Having said that, I believe that a certain degree of equivalence is maintained, the syntax in the English rendition reflecting a general disturbance of perception while the Icelandic more specifically refers to disturbance as a result of inebriation.

Pálsson never totally abandons these moments of syntagmatic reordering but they become less rare. Instead, he begins to use a kind of visual sleight of hand (mixed metaphor intended), placing something in our view, then turning it into something else. Thus 'My House' (p. 57) one of the very few poems he suggested I include, offers generous hospitality, supplying us with some material images of the house which are promptly dematerialized – leaving us to decide whether we dare enter or not.

At the other end of the scale, Pálsson is just as quick to burst the bubble of pretention, suddenly bringing everything down to earth. In 'The Acacia Tree', (p. 69) he subtly shows how a tourist guide, clearly not an expert botanist, responds to all inquiries concerning the trees that they pass with the same answer: they are acacias. Pálsson does not indicate whether the man is irritated or not by these questions, only that he occasionally pauses (to give more weight to an answer so that it appears to be considered). When the guide asks one of the tourists "what most impressed her on the trip" she answers that she was surprised at the many different kinds of acacia. What impresses me about Pálsson's account is that the satire is submerged. The truth is that, even after a recently revised division of the genus, it still comprises nearly a thousand different species. Are we then laughing at the guide, the woman tourist, the poet, or ourselves? The more I read his work, the more convinced I become that there is no fixed target for his irony, or rather that the reader may decide on the target in one reading and change it in the next.

All selections are a compromise. As I have indicated above, this task is exacerbated somewhat by choosing a handful of poems from fifteen volumes that range over almost forty years as well as by the obvious disturbance to their numerical arrangement. Indeed, making any kind of selection was the most difficult part of this endeavour as far as I was concerned. When I asked Sigurður Pálsson which poems he would prefer to have translated, he said that the matter was entirely in my hands, and it was only when I had completed the selection that he suggested, but by no means demanded, the inclusion of 'My House' and 'Plywood'. A few months after I had decided on the selection, Pálsson published his fifteenth volume of poetry, *Ljóðorkulind*, and I felt that we had to include at least one poem from it. It was then at Pálsson's suggestion that I translated 'Announcement from the International Assembly of Diamonds' (p. 133). Thus, all responsibility for this selection as well, of course, for its accuracy, rests with me. Pálsson has his own, long experience as a translator of such key writers as Fernando Arrabal, Jean Genet, Arthur Adamov, Arthur Miller, Georges Feydeau and a host of others. It is typical of the man that he retains a remarkable enthusiasm for translation and is quicker to defend its virtues than to list its shortcomings. While I, being an Englishman, naturally assumed that someone like Pálsson would have discovered many major writers through the medium of English, he informed me that the official second language of Iceland during his youth was Danish and, further, that since the Danes translated just about everything, it was through Danish that he became familiar with some of the world's greatest literature. He added, however, that he had originally read a number of important poets in Icelandic translation and that what little existed was often of a very high quality.

Although I have been translating from Icelandic to English for over thirty years, I am anything but an expert in translation theory. My intention here, as elsewhere, is to do justice to the original, but like most translators I am never entirely happy with the outcome. Icelandic is a very rich language, not perhaps in terms of vocabulary but in its grammatical structuring and the subtlety of its references to a literary past that stretches back over a thousand years. It retains, just like Attic Greek, a verbal form known as middle voice in which the subject(s) can simultaneously be the agent(s) and the object(s) of an action. In most modern languages, this is replaced by a reflexive. Thus, in French, *s'embrasser* means to kiss, making it clear grammatically that something or someone is *being* kissed. Middle voice is more economic and allows for example for something to be found (*að finnast*) without having to name the finder. *Það finnst* means something like "it will turn up" in English but other phrases using this middle voice are not as easy to transform into something recognisable. When I personalise the verb by saying *"mér finnst"* (using the dative rather than the middle voice), I am indicating that I both feel something and that I have an opinion but it is inevitably stronger in Icelandic because of its self-reflexivity. This is no place to attempt an explanation of the strengths and weaknesses of Icelandic as compared to English. I merely want to reiterate the fact that plenitude is not always indicated by words alone but also by the permutations, compressions, and associations of a language and further that there is no direct correspondence between any of the above constituent parts.

One part of the experience of being an Icelander, only alluded to above, is an identity that is rooted in the land itself and in the landscape. The Norse phrase *með lögum skal landið byggja*, still the motto of the Shetland Islands, stands at the centre of Icelandic Settlement consciousness. Literally, it means "with laws shall the land be built", an imperative that seeks to avert confrontation and insist on the need for constraint. Every Icelander knows this phrase, which is inextricably associated with their pride in the unique creation of a democracy. The *lögsögumaður* [lawspeaker], an office established in 930 at the same time as the Alþing, the first European parliament, memorised all the laws of the land, in a manner parallel to that of the bards memorising their compositions. Thus, the context for both the volume and the series entitled 'Ljóðnámuland' refers to the Settlement itself and to the book in which the settlers were recorded, *Landnámubók*. While many of Pálsson's works evince images of the streets and coffee houses of Paris or other foreign vistas in the Old and the New World, he also constantly returns to his Icelandic identity, to the Icelandic landscape and the "miracle", as he calls it, of discovering this island. I was convinced from the outset that the series 'Ljóðnámuland' had to be included here, but I also knew that it was by far the most difficult series to translate. Pálsson's compound neologism is in one sense transparent, meaning "poetry settled the land". Yet, this is also a clear allusion to "laws" settling the land and therefore suggests that the country was "civilised" by poetry. To make this association even easier for the Icelandic reader, the word for law (*lag*, pl. *lög*) also means a song (both the English word "lay" and the Icelandic *lag* deriving from the same root) and shape, position, (such as "lay" as in "the lay of the land"). At the same time, one of the many cognates of the verb *að nema* [to settle] is *náma*, which is the common Icelandic word for a "mine". I have to admit that most of these subtleties are lost in the English translation, struggling as it does to remain hinged to the original. My only consolation here is that where I am forced to diverge from the Icelandic, I am at least reiterating Pálsson's image of what is steadfast giving rein to flights of the imagination.

Finally, I would like to say something about one of the three poems that Pálsson suggested I include, the prose-poem, 'Plywood', because it so typifies a style and an attitude that permeates all of his work. Ostensibly about a school project where a boy makes a plywood 'map' of Iceland, it is also much more than that. The boy notes that drawing the outline is easy enough but that, for reasons he does not understand, he begins to saw on the opposite side of the country to where he was "situated at the time". In short, he starts at Reykjavík, which is about as far away as it is possible to be if you are in Pálsson's home territory. It transpires, though, that the decision was correct. Most of the Icelandic coast is convoluted with bays, inlets and fjords of all shapes and sizes, but the south coast (Pálsson calls it "harbourless") is fairly even in comparison and, because tackled last, allows the boy a relatively straightforward end to the task. The geographical references will not be apparent to the foreign reader who does not have a knowledge of actual locations and the cultural associations they carry, but it is apparent that those that mean most are the places his mother and father were born. By Christmas, he admits to only having reached the West Fjords and is beginning to despair of ever completing the whole thing. By spring, he has reached the south coast and finally reaches the point at which he started, Reykjavík. The reference to the weather report at the end of the poem I take as a kind of insiderism and depends somewhat on knowing not only what weather charts looked like in Iceland before the invention of the blue screen but also of the content of the weather report. The glancing reference to Robert Frost's 'Out, out...', itself a reference to *Macbeth*, is more a tremor than a resonance since the tragedy in this instance is avoided. The young boy looks up and nearly breaks a blade, but more importantly to him he nearly ruins the "line" he has drawn. This plywood Iceland and the memory of making it give rise to a flood of associations, leading from difficulty to joy but tempered in the end by the smell of the plywood and the sawdust, a bitter-sweet memory. I am already guilty here of over-explication, but rest assured that I have not even begun to look at the shapes of meaning in this poem. The most important thing I have learned from Sigurður Pálsson is to trust the reader.

Martin S. Regal

INSIDE VOICES, OUTSIDE LIGHT

úr
LJÓÐ VEGA MENN
(1980)

NOCTURNES HANDA SÓLKERFINU

Nocturne handa Merkúr

Innri raddir
Ljós að utan
Snertipunktur

Speglun og vitneskja
um einingu
í brothættri mynd
í andvaragáruðum spegli vatnsins

Speglun og vitneskja
um einingu
í hverfulli mynd
á mjóum speglunum í salnum

Orðanna hljóðan og innri raddir
Hið kvika silfur og ljós að utan
í brothættum hverfulum snertipunkti

from
POEM WAY MEN
(1980)

NOCTURNES FOR THE SOLAR SYSTEM

Nocturne for Mercury

Inside voices
Outside light
Interface

Reflection and knowledge
of unity
in a fragile image
in the ruffled mirrors of water

Reflection and knowledge
of unity
in a fleeting image
in the narrow mirrors in the hall

Fractions of words and voices within
Quick silver itself light without
fragile fleeting interface

Nocturne handa Venus

Stytta í garðinum ljósið tæplega blátt
Vindurinn hvergi nærri fremur en orðin
Samt eru einhverjar raddir ofnar í trén

Grátandi berdreymin kona
og einasta mennska ljósið er milt og gult
Vindurinn hvergi nærri fremur en orðin

Nocturne handa Fullu Tungli

Á leiðinni yfir torgið
úlpuklædd hlæjandi samloka
Bæði nokkuð við tungl

Nóttin byggir hlýjar borgir:
bogagöng súlur hvelfingar
Nóttin líka nokkuð við tungl

Úlpuklædd bogagöng við torgið
hlæjandi samloka hvelfingar
Tunglið á leiðinni

NOCTURNE FOR VENUS

A statue in the garden the light just blue
The wind no nearer than the words
Even so certain voices woven in the trees

Crying visionary woman
and the only human light is soft and pale gold
The wind no nearer than the words

NOCTURNE FOR A FULL MOON

On their way across the square
laughing, joined at the hip in an anorak
Both a little touched by the moon

The night builds warm cities
arches columns domes
The night also a little touched by the moon

Anoraked arching by the square
A dome, joined at the hip, laughing
The moon on its way

NOCTURNE HANDA PREIFANDI FULLU TUNGLI

Jassmennirnir blása næturgalnir berja
hella tónolíu á eldinn
Blóðheitur hvirfilvindur um gólfið

Skýlaust tunglið blindfullt leikur á banjó
Þöglar hamraborgarstaðreyndir í skildagatíð
vinda sér trompettmálóðar í nútíð

Og jassmennirnir blása næturgalnir berja
hella tónolíu á eldinn
Emjandi strengir leiftrandi málmur

Og áfram jassinn næturgalinn
Kviknakin hrynjandi
Dumbrautt háflæði ástríðuþrár

NOCTURNE HANDA MARS

Ryðgaður í framan í rauðlýsinu móður
rauður eins og hættan og lífið
Sannleikur málmsins sagður
rauður eins og ástúð eldfjallsins
grimmd jarðarinnar
í vitorði með tímaleysinu
í vöggu í gröf

Ryðgaður í framan í rauðlýsinu móður
rauður og hás eins og sveittur tryllitæknir
á ískrandi blikkdós
Framljósum beint útí rauðan buskann
Afturljósum rauðum frammí dauðann

Nocturne for a Brimful Moon

The jazz players blow the nightjars hammer
pour oil tones onto the flames
Hot-blooded whirlwind around the floor

The cloudless brimful moon plays the banjo
Silent precipitating facts in the conditional mood
winding straight into frenetic horns in the present tense

The jazz players blow the nightjars hammer
pour oil tones onto the flames
Whining strings glittering metal

And still jazz the nightjar beats
Stark naked rhythms
Crimson high tide of passionate longing

Nocturne for Mars

Rusty-faced and out of breath in the red glow
red like danger like life
The truth of the metal reported as
red as the compassion of the volcano
cruelty of the earth
conspiring with timelessness
in a cradle in a grave

Rusty-faced in the red glow
red and hoarse the sweating fast-lane specialist
in a screeching rattletrap
Headlights straight out into the red void
Red rearlights forward into Death

NOCTURNE HANDA JÚPÍTER

Brosmildir tónar
Marglit ljósker
og hátíðaskap

Blátt rökkur
Bjartsýnn hringdans
um hringleikahúsið feita

Vistarverur margar
og engan sundlar
þó ekki sé ljóst í dauflýsinu

hvort húsið feita snýst
eða dansararnir vænu

NOCTURNE HANDA SATÚRNUSI

Lampinn grætur
ljóshærðum tárum
Spilin á borðinu
tungan stirð
Reykurinn enn í loftinu
(alltaf hálfopnar dyr)
Gler í rúðum myrkur
bíll fer hjá
síðan þögn aftur
Lampinn grætur ekki lengur
þögn
enginn reykur
engin skýring

NOCTURNE FOR JUPITER

Easy-smiling tones
Multicoloured lantern
a mood of celebration

Blue dusk
Cheerful dance in rings
around the fat pleasure-ground

Multichambered
and no one's head spins
though it is not clear in the fading light

whether the fat house turns
or the friendly dancers

NOCTURNE FOR SATURN

The lamp cries
blond tears
The cards on the table
the tongue immobilized
The smoke still in the air
(always a half-open door)
Panes in windows darkness
a car passes
then silence once more
The lamp cries no longer
silence
no smoke
no explanation

Spilin á borðinu
engar vofur á ferli
(hálfopnar dyr alltaf)
Löngu runnin
ljóshærðu tárin

NOCTURNE HANDA ÚRANUSI

Í ljóslifandi myrkri og einveru
eða hrævareldi fjölveru
vex frelsissprotinn brunaslönguþaninn

Og skyndilega berast
næsta ótrúlegar fréttir
Hipsumhaps hvernig fer
eða hvað gerist næst

Írafár hreyflanna í flugtaki
Víðsýnisfiðringurinn
á einni bylgjunni þrungin þögn
á þeirri næstu skarpmildir fiðlutónar

Og vetfangi síðar
næsta ótrúlegar fréttir
Hipsummál og hapsumfár
hvernig fer eða hvað
gerist næst halló!

Óðamála þulir
og írafár tangósöngvarans
eða óðaogírafellsmóratjúllað þungavigtarrokk

Hips og haps og vex
Frelsissprotinn brunaslönguþaninn

The cards on the table
no ghosts on the prowl
(a half-open door always)
Long since spent
the blond tears

NOCTURNE FOR URANUS

In the vivid midst of darkness itself and solitude
or in Saint Elmo's fire ominous in plenitude
grows freedom's wand distending fire hose

And suddenly arrives
the almost unbelievable news
Hocus pocus how's it going
hocus pocus what's on next

Frenzy of propellers at take-off
Panoramic stomach-tingling view
on one wavelength in swollen silence
on the next the hard-soft tones of a violin

And an instant later
the almost unbelievable news
Hocus-talk and pocus-woe
how's it going
what's next hello!

Frantic announcers
and the frenzy of the tango singer
or the crazy-fazey-helter-skelter-heavy-metal-rock

Hocus pocus freedom's wand
the fire hose distends and grows

LJÓÐNÁMULAND

I

Ofríkið græddi í okkur ljónshjarta
Hvergi var lengur vettvangur okkar né tún
Flóttinn mesta hetjudáðin

II

Flotinn flaut og sjóndeildin einhæf
Fljóta
Berast
Reka
Bara fljóta
Innan hringsins eilífa
Sökkva ekki

III

Hrafnar flugu úr huga okkar frjálsir
Súlur svömluðu
með rótfestu okkar alsetta verndarorðum

Súlur og hrafnar:
Boginn og örvarnar
Tréð og söngur fuglanna
Staðfestan og hugarflugið

LAND POSSESSED BY POEMS

I

Tyranny bred in us a lion's heart
No longer any field for action or for crop
Flight the most heroic act

II

The fleet floating and horizon unchanged
Afloat
Borne
Adrift
Merely floating
Within the circle of eternity
Unsinking

III

The ravens flew free from our thoughts
The pillars of rank swirled
our roots studded with spells of protection

Pillars and ravens
Bow and arrows
Tree and birdsong
The fixed gives rein to flight

IV

Kraftaverkið:
Óendanlegur
hringur sjóndeildar
tekur enda!
Við hrökkvum upp
af sjávarvímunni:
Landsýn!

V

Landslagið
Landslögin

Landslag skal byggja
Með landslögum byggja

Ný fjöll og nýir staðir
Óskrifaðar arkir
Kitlandi hugsun:
Hér á ég heima
Þetta landslag mun fylgja mér
á efsta degi
Héðan verða
minningar

Nú er að lifa!

IV

The miracle:
The unending
circle of the horizon
comes to an end!
We start up
from our sea trance:
Land!

V

The lay of the land
the laws of the land

The lay of the land shall be settled
With the land's law

New mountains and new places
Unwritten manuscripts
Thought-provoking:
Here is my home
This landscape will be with me
until the last day
From here emanate
memories

Now is the time to live!

VI

Sköpun úr óskapnaði:
gefa nafn
þiggja land og gæði
yrkja
fara eldi um landnám

Helga landið
eldljóðinu síkvika

Minnast rótanna myrku
og hins djúpa brunns

VII

Eldinum fengin bólfesta
í bústað okkar

Hvort heldur er
á fyrsta vorkvöldi
eða síðasta haustmorgni
horfum við í eldinn:
bjartur galar haninn
fagurrauður og glaður

Raddirnar hverfast í söng

VI

Creation from the inchoate:
give name
receive land and fortune
compose
settle boundary with fire

Sanctify the land
eternal kindling of fire-poems

Memory of the roots of darkness
and the deep well

VII

The fire-brand finds its resting place
in our hearth

Whether it be
the first night of spring
or the last morning of autumn
we look into the fire:
brightly crows the cockerel
handsome red and joyful

The voices disappear into song

VIII

Að austan komið
að vestan komið
að sunnan komið
alsjáandi vatnið
í djúpum brunni
í dulinni lind
nærir myrkar rætur

XI

Íbyggnir horfa gluggar
í fjórar höfuðáttir
og aðrar fjórar
milliáttir
Reisuleg ljóð
næstum því íbúðarhæf

Ljóma slær á jökulinn kraftmikla
útum norðvesturgluggann

Ljóma slær á ljóðnámuna kraftmiklu
og ljóðnámuland okkar

er ljóð námu land okkar

VIII

Come from the east
come from the west
come from the south
ubiquitous the water
in deep wells
in secret brooks
nourishing dark roots

XI

Silent the windows face
all four cardinal points
and the four mid-points
that divide them
Stately poems
almost possible to inhabit

A gleam of light strikes the powerful glacier
from the northwest window

A gleam of light strikes our mine of treasures
our land deeply veined with poems

and poems possess our land

I

Nú rása blikkkálfarnir
um göturnar
Kominn föstudagur
á hausti
Vor í lofti
á götunum við ríkin

II

Lengi lifir
í gömlum glóðaraugum
flugvallarins
Flugvélarnar löngu farnar
Árin löngu liðin

III

Þær eru dökkar
Dökkar kexkökurnar
á fangelsisþakinu

IV

Ljósvakin miðborg
milli vonar og miðmorguns
Víxlar falla og rísa upp
Aðrir ganga um gólf
Musterin standa
sterkari en sinnep

DOWNTOWN IN REYKJAVIK CITY

I

Now the tin lizzies
race around the streets
Friday's here
autumn
Spring in the air
on the streets by the liquor store

II

Still lingering
the shiners
of the old airport
The aircraft long gone
The years long past

III

They are dark
Dark biscuits
on the prison roof

IV

Woken by the light the city centre
between hope and midmorning
Securities fall and rise
Others pace the floor
The temples stand
stronger than mustard

v

Klukkuna vantar fimm mínútur í
Ferkantaður rúntur unglingsáranna
minning ein
Enn snýst Útvegsbankaklukkan
hringlaga

VI

Hreyfingar fólksins úti fyrir
frostinu merktar
Á Skálanum ekur rakarinn sér
með hlátrasköllum
Allt hornið talar digrum barka
um póla
já pólatík
Sýnist sumum hvítt og svart

VII

Loftskeytamaðurinn hugsi
Skrækróma kona að austan
biður um ábót
Skálinn er allur að tæmast

VIII

Gatan er mjúk
og þurr
eftir að atómskáldin
fóru í kaffi
og sneru teskeiðunum upp

V

It's five minutes to
Our teenage years strolling round the square
only a memory
The clock on the roof of the bank still turning
in circles

VI

The movements of people outside
marked by the frost
At Skálinn, the barber rolling about
with bursts of laughter
The regulars speak authoritatively
about ticks
yes politics
Some think it's white and black

VII

The telegram operator ruminating
A shrill voiced woman from back east
asks for seconds
Skálinn is gradually fading away

VIII

The pavement is soft
and dry again
after the Atom Poets
went for a coffee break
may their teaspoons rest in peace

IX

Skrykkjóttu vinirnir
lafa enn á steypustyrktarjárninu
Sumir ganga með hatta
Aðrir flýta sér undir þakskeggin
(og er þá ógetið hinna tárvotu)

X

Undarlegir vinningar
á miðbæjartombólunni:
Koss og hlátur
söngur eða grátur
eða nótt

En alltaf er talsvert af auðum miðum

XI

Ekki selja blaðasalarnir leiðarvísa
Alltaf vantar mig leiðarlýsingu
Varnaglar halda engu skiptist
lengur

50

IX

The staggering friends
remnant rods in the ruins
Some have hats
Others hurry under the eaves
(not to mention those wet with tears)

X

Strange prizes
at the downtown raffle
A kiss and a laugh
a song and a cry
or night

But there are always quite a few losing tickets

XI

The newspaper vendors don't sell manuals
I always need direction
And there's almost no hope
for Plan B

XII

Höggmyndir stíga niður
Frakkaklæddar
Hugmyndir hlaupa upp
og niður
hringstigann á hótelinu

Að venju
er glaðværu svartsýnismönnunum
hótað verðtryggðum reikningsskilum

Óskipulögð falla tárin

XIII

Ó svefngenglar svefngenglar!
Troðnir vanmáttugu afbrýðishrati
Taliði í símann!
Hringiði ykkur saman gegn fegurðinni!

Æ svefngenglar

XII

Statues step down
Clad in overcoats
Ideas run up
and down
the spiral staircase at the hotel

As usual
the cheerful pessimists
are threatened by index-linked balance sheets

Unorganized tears fall

XIII

O sleepwalkers, sleepwalkers!
Filled with powerless jealous spittle
Speak on the phone!
Call each other to protest beauty

O sleepwalkers

úr

LJÓÐ NÁMU VÖLD
(1990)

NOKKRAR VERKLEGAR ÆFINGAR Í ATBURÐASKÁLDSKAP

1

Fara inn í Reykjavíkur Apótek og biðja um venjulega herraklippingu. Leggja áherslu á að hún eigi bara að vera venjuleg ef bið verður á þjónustu.

2

Fara inn á Aðalpósthúsið í Reykjavík og biðja um tveggja manna herbergi með baði. Taka fram að það þurfi hins vegar ekki að vera með síma. Verða undrandi að skuli ekki vera bað á herbergjunum ef afgreiðslustúlkan segist ekki hafa nein herbergi.

3

Ganga inn um aðaldyr Alþingis og biðja þingvörð mjög kurteislega að fá að tala við Lilla klifurmús. Ef þingvörðurinn kannast ekki við neinn með því nafni á að spyrja hann hvort hann sé nýbyrjaður.

4

Fara inn á Hótel Borg og fá sér sæti í veitingasalnum. Biðja um réttlæti þegar þjónninn kemur. Ef þjónninn segist ekki vera með neitt þess háttar á

from
POEM MINE POWER
(1990)

A FEW PRACTICAL EXERCISES IN EVENT POETRY

1

Go to the old Reykjavik Apothecary and ask for a short-back-and-sides. Emphasize the fact that is all that you want if there's any waiting involved.

2

Go to the main post office and ask for a double room with en suite bathroom. Point out that it does not need to have a phone.

Express your surprise that there are no en suite bathrooms available when the female attendant says they don't have any rooms at all.

3

Go in through the main door of Parliament House and ask the security guard very politely if you can have a word with Reepicheep.

If the guard says that he does not know anyone of that name, ask whether he is new to the job.

4

Go to Hotel Borg and sit down in the dining hall. Ask for justice when the waiter arrives.

If the waiter says he does not have any, point at the

að benda á myndina af Jóhannesi Jósefssyni og skora á
þjóninn að taka eina glímu.
    Þegar lögreglan kemur á að veifa Ljóð námu völd eftir
Sigurð Pálsson til sönnunar því að allt sé þetta samkvæmt
bókinni.

HÚSIÐ MITT

Það vantar næstum ekki neitt
á húsið mitt
næstum ekki neitt
Það vantar á það skorsteininn
Það venst
Það vantar á það veggina
og myndirnar á veggina
Það verður að hafa það

Það vantar ekki margt
á húsið mitt
Það vantar á það skorsteininn
Hann reykir þá ekki á meðan
Það vantar á það veggina
og gluggana
og dyrnar

En það er þægilegt húsið mitt
Gjörið svo vel
Fáið ykkur sæti
Verið ekki hrædd
Við skulum fá okkur bita
brjóta brauðið dreypa á víninu
kveikja upp í arninum

portrait of the wrestler Jóhannes Jósefsson and challenge him to a bout.

When the police arrive, wave a copy of Poems Took Power by Sigurður Pálsson and say it's all according to the book.

MY HOUSE

There's almost nothing missing
at my house
almost nothing
The chimney's missing
You'll get used to that
The walls are missing
and pictures on the walls
You just have to accept that

There is not much missing
at my house
There is no chimney
so, it can't smoke for now
There are no walls
or windows
or doors

But it's comfortable, my house
Please come in
Take a seat
Don't be frightened
Let's have a bite to eat
Break bread and sip wine
Light up a fire in the hearth

Horfa
nei dást að myndunum
á veggjunum

Gjörið svo vel
gangið inn um dyrnar
eða gluggana
ef ekki bara veggina

Look at
No
Admire the pictures
On the walls

Please come in
Walk through the door
Or the windows
If you prefer

LJÓÐLÍNUDANS
(1993)

BECKETT Á CLOSERIE DES LILAS

Grænn sveipur í trjánum útifyrir

Síðdegiskyrrð og hann situr einn
í kjarna hennar
Ég sit einn og þykist lesa
Horfi á hann
og geispandi þjóninn
og tvær konur í horninu
Þær tala stöðugt báðar í einu

Við erum fimm
Ein

Hann grannvaxinn með geislabaug
úr gullbrydduðu blýi
Arnaraugu
Bráðnandi ísmolar
hverfa í gullið viskí

Ef hann er Hamm er þjónninn Clov
hugsa ég og þær eru Nagg og Nell

Hver er ég þá?

Nei þarna standa þær upp og fara
Tala báðar í einu stöðugt á leiðinni út

Við erum þrír
Einir

BECKETT AT THE CLOSERIE DES LILAS

A green wave in the trees outside

Afternoon calm and he sits alone
at its centre

I sit alone and pretend to read
Look at him
and the yawning waiter
and two women in the corner
They speak without pause both at once

We are five
Alone

He slimly built with an aura
of gold-bordered lead
Eagle eyes
Melting ice cubes
disappear in the golden whiskey

If he is Hamm then the waiter is Clov
I think and they are Nagg and Nell

Who am I then?

No, they're standing up and leaving
Talking without pause at once on their way out

We are three
Alone

Ef hann og þjónninn
eru Vladimir og Estragon
Hver er ég þá?
Pozzo eða Lucky
eða kannski bara Godot sjálfur?

Sérkennileg niðurstaða

Ísmolarnir bráðnaðir
Arnaraugun hvarfla ekki
í kjarna síðdegiskyrrðar

Þjónninn er loksins alveg að sofna
Hrekkur upp með andfælum
þegar blaðasalinn kemur æpandi
í dyrnar
með *Le Monde*

Færir okkur síðdegisútgáfu
Le Monde

utan úr grænni birtunni

If he and the waiter
are Vladmir and Estragon
Who am I then?
Pozzo or Lucky
or maybe Godot himself?
A strange conclusion

The icecubes melted
The eagle eyes do not stray
at the centre of the afternoon calm

The waiter is finally just about to fall sleep
Wakes with a start
as the newspaper vendor arrives shouting
in the doorway
with *Le Monde*

Brings us the afternoon edition
Le Monde

out of the green light

Fyrsta verkefnið sem ég valdi í handavinnu þetta haust
var að saga út Ísland úr krossviði.

Það var auðvelt verk að gera eftirmynd af landinu með
kalkípappír á krossviðarplötuna.

Sögin var með stálbláu fíngerðu blaði og ég veit ekki af
hverju ég byrjaði í Reykjavík en ekki á hinu horninu þar
sem ég var staddur; kannski sá ég fyrir mér að Faxaflóinn
yrði auðveldur viðfangs. Það reyndist enda rétt að
undanskildum Mýrunum en ég fyrirgaf það; mamma
fæddist þar.

Snæfellsnesið reyndist sérkennilega auðvelt en
erfiðleikarnir byrjuðu fyrir alvöru á Vestfjarðakjálkanum.
Ég braut fyrsta sagarblaðið strax í Gilsfirði. Þau urðu
þónokkuð fleiri. Þegar jólafríið byrjaði var ég við
Hornbjarg. Það voru ekki eftir nema nokkur sagarblöð í
skólanum svo kennarinn pantaði fleiri.

Ég hélt hreinlega að ég kæmist aldrei alla leið. Ekki einu
sinni alla leið heim. Það fór að verða ljóst að þetta yrði eina
verkefni mitt í handavinnu þennan vetur. Þegar dag var
tekið að lengja og ugglaust verið að drekka sólarkaffi um
alla Vestfirði sór ég að gefast aldrei upp, þó ég yrði marga
vetur með þetta verkefni. Loksins þegar ég komst inn á
Húnaflóa fór að ganga betur og ég braut ekki eitt einasta
sagarblað fyrr en í Axarfirði fyrir algjöran klaufaskap
þegar ég leit uppúr verkinu, horfði út um gluggann og
hugsaði: ég er að saga hérna útifyrir og sveigði blaðið
ógætilega um leið.

Austfirðir voru erfiðir að sjá en það voru líka síðustu
stóru vandamálin svo ég sagaði léttur í bragði og hlakkaði
að komast til Hornafjarðar þar sem pabbi fæddist og
föðurættin reyndar öll meira og minna aftur í landnám.

The first woodwork project I choose to do that autumn was to saw a map of Iceland out of plywood.

It was an easy task making an outline of the country using carbon paper on a sheet of plywood.

The saw had a thin steel blue blade and I don't know why I started with Reykjavik and not on the opposite corner where I was situated at the time. Maybe I thought Faxaflói Bay would be an easy proposition. That actually turned out to be correct, with the exception of Mýrar, but I let that go. Mum was born there.

Snæfellsnes Peninsula proved to be particularly easy but major difficulties began in the West Fjords. I broke the first blade as soon as I got to Gils Fjord. There were quite a few after that. When the Christmas holidays began I was in Hornbjarg. There were only a few blades left at school so the teacher ordered some more.

I seriously believed I would never get all the way round. Not even all the way home. It began to be clear that this would be my only woodwork project that winter. As the days became longer and people all over the West Fjords undoubtedly drinking 'sun' coffee. I swore I would never give up, even if it took me many years to complete the task. Finally, when I reached Húnaflói Bay, things began to look up and I didn't break a single blade until I got to Axar Fjord and that was through sheer clumsiness when I looked up from what I was doing, glanced out the window and thought I'm not following the line here and unnecessarily bent the blade.

The East Fjords were difficult to see and that was also the last of the major obstacles so I sawed on light-heartedly and looked forward to reaching Hornafjörður where my dad was born and in fact almost the whole paternal side of my family going back as far as the Settlement.

Það var bjart yfir og fuglasöngur í lofti þegar ég rennti glaður og sigurviss eftir hafnlausri suðurströndinni. Sól skein í heiði, sauðburður var byrjaður og skólaárinu að ljúka þegar ég sagaði inn á Reykjavíkurhöfn.

Stundum þegar ég horfi á Íslandskort í veðurfregnatímum sjónvarpsins finn ég lykt af glóandi stálbláum sagarblöðum, lykt af krossviði og fíngerðu sagi.

It was a bright day and birdsong in the air when I ran happily and sure of victory across the harbourless south coast. The sun shone on the moorlands, lambing had begun and the school year was coming to a close as I sawed my way into the harbor at Reykjavik.

Sometimes when I look at a map of Iceland on the TV weather report the smell of the glowing steel saw blades comes back to me with the smell of plywood and fine sawdust.

AKASÍUTRÉ

Þeir skulu gjöra örk
af akasíuviði…
II. *Mós.* 25.10

Við höfðum lagt af stað eldsnemma um morguninn í þessa dagsferð í rútu suður við Miðjarðarhaf.

Snemma varð ljóst að leiðsögumaðurinn vissi engin deili á þeim fjölmörgu trjátegundum sem sáust út um gluggann. Alltaf sagði hann að um væri að ræða akasíutré. Stundum horfði hann vísvitandi í vitlausa átt ef spurt var um tré; leit vandlega til hægri þegar glæsileg tré blöstu við vinstra megin. Að öðru leyti virtist hann sannfróður um þá dýrðlegu hluti og staði sem við sáum á ferð okkar og áningarstöðum

Samt var sífellt haldið áfram að spyrja hann um tré og alltaf var niðurstaðan sú sama: akasíutré. Stöku sinnum tók hann sér nokkuð sannfærandi umhugsunarfrest áður en niðurstaðan var tilkynnt í hljóðnemann: þetta já… þetta sýnist mér vera… akasíutré.

Seint um kvöldið komumst við loks á áfangastað og borðuðum saman, ferðahópurinn og leiðsögumaðurinn. Talið barst að öllu því sem við höfðum séð á löngum degi.

Gömul fínleg kona hafði setið hugsi og ekki sagt aukatekið orð lengst af máltíðinni. Leiðsögumaðurinn spurði hana þá hvað væri það merkilegasta sem hún hefði séð í ferðinni.

Það merkilegasta sagði hún eftir dálitla umhugsun, það merkilegasta finnst mér hvað akasíutréð hefur mörg andlit.

THE ACACIA TREE

> And they shall make an ark
> of acacia-wood…
>   *Exodus* 25:10

We had set off at the crack of dawn in a coach on that day trip in the Mediterranean heat.

It soon became clear that our guide could not distinguish between the many different kinds of tree that we saw out of the window. He always said they were acacias and carefully looked to the right when a beautiful tree appeared on the left. In all other respects he appeared to be highly knowledgeable about the wonderful places and things that we saw both on the road and when we stopped for refreshments.

Nevertheless, there were continual questions about the trees and the outcome was always the same: an acacia. Occasionally, he paused convincingly to think before he announced his verdict over the microphone: 'that one… yes… I believe that's an acacia.'

Late in the evening we stopped and dined together, the group on the coach and the guide. We chatted about all the things we had seen that day.

An elegant elderly woman had been sitting deep in thought and had hardly uttered a word during the meal. The guide then asked what had most impressed her on the trip.

'What most impressed me?' she said after a little thought. 'What struck me most was how many different varieties of acacia there are.'

MIKLATÚN

Einar Ben í herðabreiðum frakka
með hörpu að bakhjarli
horfir beint fram
gegnum Esjuna

Skammt frá horfir höfuð
Þorsteins Erlingssonar
á Einar

Tvær styttur úr málmi
hér í þessu marmaraleysi

Og milli þeirra
leika krakkar saman
Unga Íslands merki
í litskrúðugum pollagöllum

Tvær styttur á Miklatúni
Í eyrum beggja dynjandi
fossniður umferðar

MIKLATÚN PARK

Einar Benediktsson, poet, in a wide-shouldered coat
bolstered by a harp
looks directly ahead
clean through Mt. Esja

A short distance away
a bust of Þorsteinn Erlingsson, poet
looks at Einar

Two metal sculptures
here where there is no marble

And between them
children play
'Symbols of Young Iceland'
in brightly coloured raincoats

Two statues in Miklatún
In the ears of both resound
waterfalls of traffic

úr
LJÓÐTÍMASKYN
(1999)

LEIT

Eftir endilöngum þessum vegi
Ligg ég
Ekki meðfram honum
Ég ligg
Í veginum sjálfum
Samt er ég ekki sjálfur vegurinn
Engan veginn

Ég ligg
Er að leita að þér

Og ég er í öllum þessum
Miklu vöruflutningum
Um alla veröldina
Allar þessar skrifstofur að skipuleggja
Allir þessir reikningar öll þessi föx
Allir þessir þungu gámar
Á ferð um veröldina
Draumar smyglara ég er í þeim líka
Ég er í fljótabátnum stynjandi
Á leið upp Guadalquivir
Ryðguðum krönunum
Við höfnina í Constantza
Titrandi teinum
Hraðlestarinnar Toulouse-París
Þung blaut lestin
Reynir að hreyfa sig hratt gegnum regnið

from
POEM TIME SENSE
(1999)

SEARCH

At the end of this long road
I lie
Not beside it
I lie
In the road itself
Even so, I am not the road
No way

I lie
Am looking for you

And I am in the midst
Of all this great transport of goods
Around the whole globe
All these offices organizing
All these invoices all these faxes
All these heavy containers
Travelling around the world
Dreams of smugglers I am in them too
I am in the barges gasping
Their way up Guadalquivir
Rusted cranes
At the harbour in Constantza
Trembling tracks
Of the Toulouse-Paris bullet
Heavy wet train
Trying to speed itself through the rain

En ég er alltaf að leita að þér
Öll þessi starfsemi til einskis
Ef ég finn þig ekki
Öll þessi áreynsla...

Vekjaraklukkurnar hringja
Neðanjarðarlestarnar
Renna sitt skeið
Sviði í augum af svefnleysi
Þreytu og mettuðu lofti

Öll þessi áreynsla til einskis
Án þín
Án þín sem ég bíð alla daga
Allar nætur

HIÐ SVARTA LAND

Þegar ég hafði lengi farið um hið svarta land fann ég
hvernig vegirnir þrengdust og mjókkuðu allt þar til ljóst
var að hér voru engir vegir lengur. Ekki einu sinni slóðar
né kindagötur sem ég hafði haldið mig sjá nokkru áður
við hraunjaðarinn.

Mér krossbrá við þá tilhugsun að nú yrði ég í hinu
svarta landi áfram en þá byrjuðu skyndilega dúnmjúkar
snjóflygsur að falla og héldu því viðstöðulaust áfram.
Brátt voru allir vegir færir.

But I am always looking for you
All this activity in vain
If I do not find you
All this effort…

The alarm clocks ring
The underground trains
Run their course
Eyes sore from sleeplessness
Fatigue and polluted air

All this effort in vain
Without you
Without you for whom I wait every single day
Every single night

THE BLACK LAND

When I had travelled around the black land for a long time, I felt how the roads tapered and narrowed until it was clear that there were no more roads. Not even paths or sheep trails that I thought I had seen earlier at the edge of the lava.

I was utterly taken aback at the thought I would have to stay in the black land and then suddenly some downy soft snowflakes began to fall and continued ceaselessly.

Soon all the roads were open.

LÆRDÓMAR

Öldinni lauk
með landafræðikennslu

Við lærðum
ný og ný nöfn
á landsvæðum
og borgum

Svæðum
þjóðernishreinsana
morða
borgarastyrjalda

Ný og ný nöfn
á stöðum sem var
að engu getið
í landafræðinni
í skólanum

Nú þekkjum við þessi nöfn

Ný nöfn
sem bætast við langan lista
Ný nöfn
á gamalli hlið mannsins
sem vill gleymast
í öllu framþróunartalinu:

Hinni ómennsku hlið

from
POEM TIME SEARCH
(2001)

KNOWLEDGE

The century ended
with a geography lesson

We learned
name upon new name
of regions
and cities

Regions
of genocide
murder
civil war

Name upon new name
of places that were
never mentioned
in geography
at school

Now we know these names

New names
added to a long list
New names
of man's old nature
that are forgotten
in all this talk of progress:

His inhuman nature

LJÓSASKIPTI

Við sjónhring minnisins
ljósleit segl
þanin gegnsæ

Seytlar niður
af himninum
dvínandi birta

Færist yfir himininn
færist yfir heiminn
græðandi smyrsl
rökkursins

Jórtrandi skepnur kyrrast
vindurinn kyrrist
blómin dotta

Heykvísl með gljáandi skafti
stendur vaktina

Bíður spennt

TWILIGHT

At the visible edge of memory
a light-coloured sail
full, translucent

Seeping down
from the sky
dwindling light

Spreading across the sky
across the world
the healing balm
of twilight

Grazing sheep settle
the wind settles
the flowers nod

a pitchfork with a polished shaft
stands watch

Waits poised

STJÖRNUFORM Í GRASI

Liggjandi barn
í grasi

Horfir
upp í bláleitan
óendanleika

Finnur skyndilega
punktalínur á jörðinni
allt umhverfis
liggjandi líkamann

Stjörnulaga form
teiknað með punktalínum
í svörðinn

Bláleitum
Punktalínum

STAR IN THE GRASS

A child lying
on the grass

Looks
up into the light blue
endlessness

Suddenly imagines
dotted lines on the ground
all around its
body lying there

A star-shaped form
drawn with dots
in the darkness

Light blue
Dotted lines

úr
LJÓÐTÍMAVAGN
(2003)

LJÓÐLISTIN

Fjúk og götuljósin stara niður í götuna.

Snjókorn á svelgjandi ferð og jafnharðan farin af stað aftur ef þau staldra við.

Hæggengt fjúk þar sem snjókornin falla varlega og dragast sum í uppleitan strók og hringsnúast.

Þessi hreyfing er sterkari en ég, miklu sterkari, hún er eins og ljóðlistin, lætur mig skrifa allt mögulegt, tekur af mér völdin sem betur fer.
Þannig kemur hún stöðugt á óvart. Hitt er ekki síðra að það er engu líkara en hún komi manni til sjálfs sín, heim, ef svo má segja, í einhver ný kynni, heimkynni.

Núna til dæmis lætur hún mig skrifa:

Það jarðbundnasta af öllum skáldskap er líklega ljóðlistin.

from
POEM TIME WAGON
(2003)

THE ART OF POETRY

A flurry and street lights staring down in the street.

Snowflakes scurrying along and suddenly up and away if they tarry.

A slow flurry where some fall tentatively and others are sucked into a column swirling upwards in spirals.

This movement is stronger than me, much stronger. It is like the art of poetry, has me write whatever comes to mind, takes over from me, fortunately.
That is how it constantly surprises. Even better, it is as if it brings one back to oneself, home – if one may phrase it like that – into some new relationship with oneself.

Now, for example, it has me write:

The most down-to-earth of all arts is probably poetry.

HÓTELSALUR

Ég þori ekki að segja ykkur hvar ég sit, þori það ekki.
Þori ekki að nefna þetta hótel á nafn, óttast að það
hverfi þá kannski eins og Café Hressó, Iðnaðarbankinn,
Eros Hafnarstræti og allt hitt sem er horfið...
Allt þetta sem rataði í ljóð og er horfið í
raunveruleikanum.
Ég vil ekki að þessi hótelsalur hverfi úr
raunveruleikanum.

Ég ætla ekki að segja nafnið; jafnvel við yfirheyrslur,
strangar fyrstu annarrar þriðju gráðu yfirheyrslur hjá
norðangarranum, svörtu regninu, ryðguðu járni, brotnum
gangstéttum, þá myndi ég ekki segja nafnið á þessu hóteli.

Ég sit þar núna í hótelsalnum til alls vís.

RÚÐUR

Rúðurnar á veitingahúsinu eins og speglar að utan,
sést ekkert inn.
Þeir sem inni sitja geta horft á mig en ég sé þá ekki.
Fór að gera það að venju að ganga þarna framhjá
síðdegis. Ímyndaði mér fólkið sem sat innan við rúðurnar,
sumir kannski glottandi að okkur sem keifuðum þarna
grunlaus á gangstéttinni.

Einn góðan veðurdag þoldi ég ekki meir og snaraðist
inn.
Í anddyrinu var einhvers konar dyravörður. Hann
virtist með störu eins og hann væri að fylgjast með
hættulegum manni í fjarskanum. Kannski var hann bara
að bíða eftir leigubíl sem einhver hafði pantað.

84

HOTEL LOUNGE

I dare not tell you where I am sitting. Dare not.
I dare not mention this hotel by name, am afraid that
it will become defunct like Skalli, Iðnaðarbankinn, Eros
Hafnarstræti and all those other places that are gone...

All that finds its way into poems is lost to reality.
I do not want this hotel lounge to disappear from
reality.

I am not going to say the name, not even if interrogated,
serious first- second- third-degree interrogation in vicious
northerly wind, black rain, rusted iron, broken pavements,
I still would not utter the name of this hotel.

I am sitting there now in this hotel lounge, ready for
anything.

WINDOWS

The windows at the restaurant are mirrors from the
outside, no seeing in.
Those sitting inside can see me but I cannot see them.
Made a habit of walking past in the afternoon. Imagined
the people sitting by the windows, some of them perhaps
smirking at us trudging about unsuspectingly on the
pavement.

One fine day I could not stand it anymore and I rushed
inside.
In the lobby was some kind of doorman. He appeared to
be staring ahead as if he were keeping close watch on some
dangerous individual in the distance. Perhaps he was simply
looking out for a cab that someone had ordered.

Salurinn var talsvert stærri en ég hafði haldið en þar voru miklu færri en ég hafði ímyndað mér.

Ekki var setið nema við tvö borð. Við hringborðið í horninu sátu menn sem gátu verið lögfræðingar og hrukkótt kona við lítið borð nálægt innganginum. Enginn sat við öll borðin sem vissu út að gangstéttinni sem voru samt ákjósanlegur staður til að fylgjast með fólki ganga hjá.

Ég ákvað að setjast við eitt gluggaborðanna. Enginn kom að afgreiða mig. Svo var allt í einu dregið niður í ljósunum í salnum, líklega með þessu apparati sem kallað er dimmer. (Kannski heitir það eitthvað annað en að minnsta kostir dimmir þegar honum er snúið.)

Það sljákkaði skyndilega í mannskapnum við hringborðið þegar dofnaði lýsingin. Engu líkara en dimmerinn stjórnaði raddstyrknum að minnsta kosti í nokkrar mínútur.

Konan í horninu titraði aðeins í skjóli dimmunnar eins og hún hafi haldið niðrí sér hrolli lengi.

Nú bar svo við að ég sá alls ekki lengur neitt út um gluggana, sá enga umferð á gangstéttunum. Engar augljósar hrukkur voru lengur framan í konunni við litla borðið.

Þá var hvíslað að mér, skýrt og greinilega, eins og einhver stæði rétt hjá mér:

– Bráðum…

The dining area was considerably larger than I had thought but there were far fewer people than I imagined.

Only two tables were occupied. At a round table in one corner sat a group of men who could have been lawyers, and a woman with wrinkles sat at a small table near the entrance. No one was sitting at any of the tables that faced the street, which was the ideal place to watch passers by.

I decided to sit down by one of the window tables. No one came to attend to me. Then, suddenly, all the lights went down, probably done with a dimmer switch. (Maybe it's called something else but that's what it does.)

Then the group at the round table suddenly went quiet as the lights faded, as if the switch controlled the volume of their voices, at least for a couple of minutes.

The woman in the corner trembled in the refuge of the dark as if she had been repressing a shudder for some time.

Then it transpired that I could not see a thing out of the windows any longer, saw no one passing by on the pavement. There were no longer any obvious wrinkles on the face of the woman at the little table.

Some one whispered to me, loud and clear, as if standing right beside me:

'Soon...'

LJÓSMYND AF LÁTNU BARNI

Barnið í örmum sorgarinnar og sorgin ein lifir.
Lifir ein áfram í dauðabliki ljósmyndar.

Stimplar sorgina áfram eins og biluð prentvél andstætt
hreyfimyndunum í sjónvarpinu þar sem aldrei er dauður
punktur í miðjum ofbeldisdauðanum.

Aldrei kyrr punktur þar sem sorgin ein lifir.

SITJUM ÁFRAM

Sitjum áfram
lesum blöðin
af veðurbitnu tré heimsins

Dagarnir setjast í hár okkar
dagarnir líða undir lok
grána
detta af
eins og stórveldi

Og nóttin kemur og við bíðum
vonum að andardrátturinn
verði jafnari
bíðum eftir nýrri dagsbrún

logni óveðri
nýjum ógnum

Sitjum áfram
lesum blöðin
af veðurbitnu tré heimsins

PHOTOGRAPH OF A DEAD CHILD

The child in the arms of grief and only grief living.

Living on in the dead instant of the photograph.

Presses grief forward like a broken printer quite opposite to the moving pictures on the television where there is never a stillborn moment in the middle of all those violent deaths.

Never a calm point where only grief lives.

KEEP ON SITTING HERE

Let's keep sitting
leafing through what is shed
from the weatherbeaten tree of the world

The days settle in our hair
days end in the end
greying
falling from
like a super power

And the night comes and we wait
hope that our breathing
will be more even
wait for the brink of a new day

the storm to calm
new threats

Let's keep sitting
leafing through what is shed
from the weatherbeaten tree of the world

HROKI

Þarf svo líka
að hlusta á ævisögur
hinna föllnu
í liði sigurvegaranna

Sögur af hetjum
og hetjudáðum

Þarf virkilega
að sitja hér endalaust
undir mærð
sigurvegaranna

ofan á allt annað

Mærðin
þessi nauðgun
tilfinninganna

sem reynir alltaf að breyta
stolti

í hroka

ARROGANCE

Also need
to listen to the life stories
of the fallen
in the ranks of the victorious

Stories of heroes
and heroic deeds

Absolutely need
to sit here indefinitely
subject to the bombast
of the victors

on top of everything else

The bombast
this rape
of the emotions

that always turns
pride

into arrogance.

MIÐNÆTTI

Höggva sér leið
Kominn tími
Klukkan að verða ferð

Kominn tími til
að höggva sér leið
gegnum skóginn

Atkvæði fyrir atkvæði
Átta sig á nóttinni
bak við hvert einasta tré

Engir fuglar syngja
í nóttinni

Kominn tími
Klukkan að verða
klukkan að verða ferð

Inn og út

from
POEM ENERGY FIELD
(2006)

MIDNIGHT

Hack themselves a path
The time come
The clock becomes a journey

The time come
to hack themselves a path
through the forest

Syllable by syllable
Comprehends night
behind every single tree

No birds sing
in the night

The time come
The clock becomes
the clock becomes a journey

in and out

Í ÞAKSKEGGINU

Upp úr miðnætti
skelfur tíminn
eitt augnablik

Þessi örstutti tímaskjálfti
snarpur ósýnilegur hrollur

fyllir húsið mitt
af dúfum

Þær segja mér sögur
þannig veit ég af þeim

En þær sjást ekki
jafnvel skyggnasta fólk
hefur aldrei séð þær

Veit ekkert hvar þær halda sig
ímynda mér stundum
að þær sitji í þakskegginu

En þær segja mér sögur
á hverri nóttu

eftir að örstuttur tímaskjálfti
hefur fyllt húsið mitt
af dúfum

IN THE EAVES

Just after midnight
time trembles
for an instant

This brief timequake
an abrupt invisible shudder

fills my house
with pigeons

They tell me stories
that's how I know about them

But they cannot be seen
not even clairvoyants
have ever seen them

Do not know where they linger
I imagine sometimes
that they sit in the eaves

But they tell me stories
every night

after a very brief timequake
has filled my house
with pigeons

FESTINGIN

Festingin í morgunmyrkri
blasir við tindrandi
í miðmorgunmyrkri

svonefnd festing
fullkomlega laus
við festingu

laus og liðug
tindrandi festing

opnar okkur
nýtt skynsvið
nýtt orkusvið

ljóðorkusvið

EKKERT

Ekkert...

hve frjálsar virðast mér setningar
sem hefjast á þessu orði!

ekkert...

ég dái þetta orð
dýrka þessa fagnaðarstunu
þessa hvítu örk

þetta orð sem minnir á stundina
rétt fyrir dögun

THE FIRMAMENT

The firmament in morning darkness
appears sparkling
in the midmorning darkness

what we call the firmament
absolutely free
of firmness

loose and fancy free
the sparkling firmament

reveals to us
a new field of perception
a new energy field

an energy field of poetry

NOTHING

Nothing...

how free they seem to me,
sentences that begin with this word!

nothing...

I love that word
adore this welcoming sigh
this white stack of paper

that word that reminds me of the moment
just before dawn

ekkert...

ekkert vald óttast ég
ekkert göngulag hef ég tileinkað mér

Draga svefninn
þennan ónýta jaxl
fumlaust úr nóttinni

án deyfingar
endilega án deyfingar

Draga kengboginn nagla væntinganna
úr myrkrinu

Framundan enn og aftur
hringrás fæðing
endurfæðing

MYRKRIÐ

Og myrkrið leitar og finnur
ljóð sem situr í myrkrinu
erfitt að greina hvar

nákvæmlega hvar
í salnum og hljómsveitin
sést vitanlega ekki heldur

Fyrir utan
er blátt tunglskin sem heldur
varlega utan um myrkrið

nothing…

nothing has the power to frighten
no special gait have I made my own

Pull sleep
that rotten tooth
deftly from the night

with no anaesthetic
absolutely anaesthetic

Pull that twisted nail of expectation
out of the dark

Ahead once more
cycle birth
rebirth

THE DARK

And the dark looks and finds
a poem that sits in the dark
difficult to say where

exactly where
in the auditorium and the orchestra
cannot be seen either, naturally

Outside
is blue moonlight that carefully
enfolds the dark

Blátt tunglskin sem hlustar
á andardrátt okkar
og hljómsveitarinnar

Og myrkrið heldur áfram
að leita og finna
ljóð sem situr í myrkrinu

EILÍFI MORGUNN

Dökkir glansandi skuggar
á málverkinu
eru ekki nóttin

Dökkir glansandi skuggar
eru djúpir kossar
án orða

Djúpir kossar
svört sundlaug
lokaðra augna

Þéttingsfastar grímur
loksins lausar af andlitunum
Hver ertu?

Megum ekki vita það
Verðum bara að halda áfram
með lokuð augun

Blue moonlight that listens
to our breathing
and to that of the orchestra

And the dark continues
to search and find
a poem that sits in the dark

ETERNAL MORNING

Dark glistening shadows
on the painting
are not the night

Dark glistening shadows
are deep kisses
without words

Deep kisses
black swimming pool
of closed eyes

Tightly gripping masks
finally free of the faces
Who are you?

We may not know that
We just have to continue

with eyes closed

BROTASÝN

Ljómun
Brotasýn
Umbreyting

Verk mitt mósaík
mynd á engum vegg

Reika um götur borganna
reika
með opnum huga inn í sýn
sem verður til
inni fyrir úti fyrir
verður til með hreyfingunni

Óttinn við skort
á heild
hefur aldrei gagntekið mig

Nakin snörp og stundum
allt að því harkaleg
gleðivíma á auðu blaði

Annars vegar
og hins vegar...

og báðir vegir álíka færir
eða ófærir

Annars vegar
að skrifa
ekki neitt framar
ekki hreyfa neitt
forðast...
Þetta hef ég reynt

FRAGMENTED VIEW

Illumination
Visible fragment
Transformation

My work a mosaic
a picture on no wall

Strolling about the city streets
strolling
with a mind open to a view
that comes into being
on the inside on the outside
comes into being with the motion

The fear of shortage
on the whole
has never captivated me

The naked sudden and sometimes
almost brutal
intoxication of joy at a blank sheet

On the one hand
and on the other…

and both ways equally passable
and impassable

On the one hand
never to write
anything again
not move anything
avoid…
I have tried that

Hins vegar
finn ég kitlandi spennu
dýpst í djúpi
líkamans

finn fyrir hreyfingunni
finn fyrir henni og veit
ekki fyrr
en ég er kominn af stað

farinn að leita veit ekki
hvert hún leiðir mig
þessi hreyfing

Enn eina ferðina
um opna vegi
auðar síður
en alltaf

alltaf eins og þetta verði
í síðasta skipti
í lífinu

Þetta verði
síðustu skilaboðin

Þannig hefur það verið
og báðir vegir álíka færir
eða ófærir

Enn og aftur:

Þetta eru síðustu skilaboðin

On the other hand
I feel a stirring of excitement
deep in the depths
of my body

feel a movement
feel it and know
not until
I have started out

gone to look I know not where
wherever it leads me
this motion

One more journey
on the open road
empty pages
but always

Always the same and this will be
the last time
in my life

This will be
the last message

That is how it has been
and both ways equally passable
and impassable

Once again:

This is the last message

ANDARTAK

Að finna fyrir gleði
í hverjum andardrætti

Það er eina alvarlega skyldan
í lífinu
(um dauðann fullyrði ég ekkert)

Endurtek þessa helgun
á tímanum
í miðri afhelgunarskyldunni

Ég er að tala um
nýja helgun
á hverju einasta andartaki

sem afhelgast ekki fyrr
en við öndum frá okkur

LJÓSIÐ

Ljósið fellur ekki
og hefur aldrei gert

Það er með sterkari vængi
en hásir mávarnir

Ljósið tekur sífellt á sig
nýjar myndir:

Þanin segl
við sjónarrönd
Glitrandi bergvatn
Andardráttur í svartamyrkri

EACH BREATH

To feel joy
in every breath

That is the only real imperative
in life
(about death I assert nothing)

Repeat this consecration
of time
in the midst of desecration

I am talking about
a new consecration
in each and every breath

that is not desecrated before
we breathe out again

LIGHT

Light does not fall
and never has

It has stronger wings
than the rasping seagulls

Light always takes on
new shapes

A full sail
at the horizon's edge
Glistening mountain water
Breathing in black darkness

Ljósið fellur ekki
og hefur aldrei gert

Það streymir stöðugt
innan frá

SKUGGINN

Þar sem ég sit í horninu
fellur skugginn af mér
á blaðið

Ljósið er á veggnum
aftan við mig

Vil ekki að skugginn
komi á blaðið

skugginn af sjálfum mér
þegar ég skrifa

Þegar ég settist hér inn
flæddi sólin
niður í þröngt strætið

Einu ljóði síðar
flæðir regn
niður í þröngt strætið

Allt annað
allt annað stræti
þar sem ég eitt sinn var

Light does not fall
and never has

It streams continually
from within

THE SHADOW

Where I sit in the corner
my shadow falls on
the page

The light is on the wall
behind me

Do not want the shadow
on the page

my own shadow
when I write

When I sat down in here
the sun flooded
along the narrow street

one poem later
the rain floods
down the narrow street

Utterly different
an utterly different street
where I once was

Er ekki
er ekki lengur

FRELSIÐ ER SPURN

Frelsið er spurn

Örlítið bil
milli þín og heimsins

Í þetta
bil

í þessa
eyðu

má gróðursetja spurn
á að gróðursetja
verður að

gróðursetja spurn

Am not
am no longer

FREEDOM IS A QUESTION

Freedom is a question

A tiny gap
between me and the world

In this
gap

In this
space

one may plant a question
should plant
must

plant a question

Á hverjum morgni vaxa vængir á ljónið á stöplinum.
En þessi myndbreyting er ekki bara breyting á mynd.
Þar byrjar þetta.
Allt.
Á hverjum morgni.

Þegar vængirnir hafa vaxið á ljónið fer spurningum
fjölgandi. Svörunum fækkar.
Tsimm-tsúmm. Þú veist ekki hvað það þýðir? Þá er að
leita svara. Tsimm-tsúmm.
Einn verður tveir.
Tveir taka tal saman.

Við sem höfum aldrei talað saman, tölum saman.
Núna.
Að gleðjast yfir hverjum andardrætti er ekki bara
eitthvað aukaatriði, ábyrgðarlaus setning út í loftið.
Það er skylda.
Lífsgleðin er skylda sem er jafnframt gleði eins og
nafnið bendir til.
Ofsinn að lifa er nauðsyn, lífsnauðsyn. Skyldan að
standa gegn hvers kyns alræði. Uppreisn.

Ljóðlistin er nauðsyn.
Gleði.
Ofsi.
Uppreisn.

Lífsnauðsyn og lífsgleði.
En hún er ekki neins konar félagsleg nauðsyn.

Þarna hafið þið það.

112

Every morning, the wings on the lion on the column grow. But this metamorphosis is not simply visual.
There it begins.
Everything.
Every morning.

When the wings have grown on the lion, the questions begin to multiply. The number of answers decreases.

TsimTsum. You don't know what that means? Then answers have to be sought. TsimTsum.

One becomes two.
Two take to speaking together.

We, who have never spoken, speak to each other.
Now.

To thrill at each breath is not simply some minor detail, an irresponsible remark.
It is an imperative.
The joy of life is an imperative that is also a joy, as the phrase indicates.
The rage to live is necessary, vital. The imperative to stand against any kind of tyranny. Revolt.

The art of poetry is necessary.
Joy.
Rage.
Revolt.

Vitally necessary and the joy of life.
But no kind of social necessity.

And there you have it.

Drífa sig út að berja tréð. Lumbra á því fram að hádegi. Ekkert kemur. Enginn ávöxtur.

Skráningin vitlaus eða hvað? Safinn ekki að virka?

Eftir hádegishléð er orðið of heitt að lumbra...

Síðdegi.
Ekki mikil breyting. Lumbrað á trénu. Trjástofninn sofandi? Hvað veit maður.

Sortnar fyrir augum í funhitanum sem lumbrar á manni. Dvöl.
Pása.

Hlýir skuggar koma loks með kennsluefnið: teygja sig eftir ávöxtunum, bara teygja sig eftir ávöxtunum...

ÓÐUR

Áður...
Það var áður. Þegar sólin þurfti að þrengja sér inn um gluggann, þegar pípureykurinn olli heyrnarleysi. Nei, það er ekki satt.
Hið sanna í málinu er að ég var að enduruppgötva ástina. Kossar þeirra! Kossar fólksins á næsta borði.

Og það er sjöundi júlí í dag. Undarlegt!
Þetta gerist sama dag og ég uppgötvaði hina röddina. Þessa sem er innra með mér og komst þess vegna út fyrir mig.

Samtölin! Samtölin við þetta borð.

BOLE

Hurry outside and hit that tree. Beat it until lunchtime. Nothing will happen. No fruit.

Wrong docket, perhaps? The sap not working?

After lunch it will be too hot to beat anything…

Afternoon.
Not much change. Beating the tree. The bole asleep? Who knows?

Everything goes black in the excessive heat that beats down on me. Stay.
Pause.

Finally, warm shadows bring the teaching materials; stretch out for the fruit, just stretch out for the fruit…

ODE

Earlier…
It was earlier. When the sun needed to cram itself in through the window, when the smoke from the pipe caused general deafness. No, that's not true.
The truth of the matter is that I had rediscovered love. Their kisses! The kisses of the couple at the next table.

And it's 7 July today. Very strange!
This happened the same day as I discovered the other voice. The one that is inside me and emerged for me as a result.

The conversations! The conversations at that table.

Þetta hlýlega kaffihús með fallegum glansandi dökkbrúnum tréborðum sem hafa nú örugglega heyrt annað eins. Heldur betur. Hér hafa snillingar setið.

En að þetta skyldi gerast sama dag, er það ekki óvenjulegt, jafnvel ótrúlegt? Sama stund og það sem meira er, sami staður. Því er til að svara, að þetta gerðist samhliða, kannski ekki endilega sama dag á almanakinu. Og tréborðin þau sömu. Hér standa þau vaktina, hlið við hlið, mynda trausta röð eins og dagarnir, stundirnar, staðirnir.

Áður verður óður.
Óður sem er tilbúinn að taka á móti lífinu.
Óður til dýrðar þeirra samtala sem halda áfram til eilífðar við glansandi dökkbrúnu tréborðin.
Samhliða.

GAMLA HÖFNIN

Svona hefði aldrei getað gerst við nýju höfnina. Það er bara við gamlar hafnir sem annað eins gerist.

Fyrst fóru skipin að minnka smám saman. Ekkert voðalega hratt en örugglega án þess að nokkurt lát yrði á.

Það var skringilegt að sjá hvernig mennirnir á þilfarinu þurftu að læra að stíga ölduna á nýjan máta eftir því sem bátarnir fóru minnkandi.

Smábátagerið ruggaði um alla höfnina með mönnum sem héldu sumir varla jafnvægi á þessum litlu skektum.

116

That cosy café with the beautiful shiny dark brown wooden tables that have undoubtedly never heard anything like it. I'll say! Here, geniuses have sat.

But, that it should have happened on the same day, isn't that unusual, even unbelievable? At the same time and, even more amazing, in the same place.

That is to say that it happened side by side, maybe not necessarily on the calendar day.

And the wooden tables are the same. They stand watch here, side by side, forming a reliable row like the days, the hours, the locations.

Earlier becomes an ode.

The ode that is ready to embrace life.

Ode to the glory of those conversations that continue forever at the shiny dark brown wooden tables.

Side by side.

THE OLD HARBOUR

This could never have happened at the new harbour. It is only at old harbours that such things happen.

First, the ships slowly grew smaller. Not terribly fast but steadily without any pause.

It was odd to see how the men on the decks had to find their sea legs again in a new manner after the ships began to grow smaller.

The small fishing boats rolled around the entire harbour with men aboard, some of whom could hardly keep their balance on these tiny craft.

Þá fóru að koma bátar að landi, þeir voru allir af sömu stærð, aðeins stærri en skekturnar. Ákafir glaðværir sjómenn hrópuðu til okkar fagnaðarfréttir, að þeir hefðu náð í furðulega fiska sem þeir hefðu hreinlega aldrei séð áður.

Og það kom heldur betur í ljós þegar þeir komu að hafnarbakkanum. Þarna gat að líta magnaða litadýrð af spriklandi fiskum. Sterkir litir eins og fauvistar hefðu málað þá, menn sem þóttu svo snaróðir á myndfletinum að þeir voru kenndir við villidýr.

Sjómennirnir lönduðu fiskunum, sumir berir að ofan og víða glitti í tattú. Litadýrðin dreifðist yfir hafnarbakkann þar sem kvikindin lágu í kerjum en þegar þeir voru næstum búnir að tæma bátana, kom í ljós, að tattúin voru farin að dofna og það var greinilega ekkert sem gat bjargað þeim.

Meðan á löndun stóð fóru hringar á fingrum okkar á bryggjunni að stækka og undir lokin var svo komið að þeir héldust ekki á fingrunum og féllu með glamri á bryggjudekkið.

Nú komu einhver tvö kvikindi fljúgandi sem reyndust vera snæuglur. Annar fuglinn nánast alhvítur og hinn hvítur með yrjum. Greinilega kven- og karlfugl.

Við erum að koma frá Ódáðahrauni, heyrðist mér þau segja en það heyrðist ekki vel fyrir kvöldfréttunum.

Then the boats began to come ashore. They were all the same size, a little larger than the smallest craft. The eager, happy fishermen shouted out the good news, that they had caught some strange fish that they had never seen before.

And that was very obvious as they reached the wharf. There, one could see an amazing multicoloured mass of wriggling fish. Strong colours as if the Fauvists had painted them, artists whose works were considered so crazy that they were likened to wild animals.

The fishermen landed the fish. Some of the crew were naked to the waist, tattoos flashing here and there. The glorious colour spread over the wharf where the creatures lay in vats, and when they had almost emptied the boats it transpired that the tattoos were beginning to fade and it was clear that nothing could save them.

While they brought the catch ashore, we on the jetty realized that the rings on our fingers were getting bigger, and in the end they slipped off our fingers and fell to the jetty with a rattle.

Now two creatures came flying that proved to be snowy owls. One of the birds was almost completely white and the other white with speckles. Clearly, a male and a female.

'We are returning from the plain of ill deeds, Ódáðahraun,' I thought I heard them say, but the evening news smothered the sound.

LJÓÐORKUÞÖRF

II

Annaðhvort
er að drepa tímann
eða blása í hann lífi

svo hann haldi
manni á lífi

Dauður tími
er eilíflega dauður
fastur í auðri eyðu

En lifandi tíma er hægt
að endurlífga
endalaust

Eilífðarvél
knúin eldsneyti
minnisins

III

Þetta er ekki spurning um rými
nær fjær
fjær nær

Við erum að tala um tíma
Hafðu ekki áhyggjur
þótt þú sért engu nær

POEM-ENERGY-NEED

II

Either
we are killing time
or breathing new life into it

so that it
keeps us alive

Dead time
is eternally dead
trapped in empty space

But living time can be
revived
endlessly

The eternal machine
driven by the fuel
of memory

III

It is not a question of space
near far
far near

We are talking about time
Don't worry
If you're miles off

Við erum tvífarar
hittumst samt aldrei

Annar les
hinn skrifar

Hittumst aldrei
aldrei
tvífarafjandar
tvífaraskrattar

Köstum steinum úr glerhúsi
eða gleri úr steinhúsi
Fer eftir stemningunni

Tvífarar erum við
Finnum það

Báðir
báðir

IV

Slagorð
Áróður
Væmni
Mærð

Ekkert af þessu
takk fyrir
Hvað þá?

Texta
ljóðtexta
bókmenntatexta
Ekkert annað

We are doubles
though we never meet

One reads
the other writes

We never meet
never
twin foes
twin devils

Throwing stones from glass houses
or glass from stone houses
Depends on the mood

We are doubles
We can feel it

Both of us
Both of us

IV

Slogans
Propaganda
Syrupy
Sentimentality

None of these
Thank you
What then?

Writing
Poetry
Literature
Nothing else

Vil hvorki öskra né þegja
né hlýða

Skáldskaparvaldið
Eina valdið sem ég undirgengst

Hef aldrei viljað öskra né þegja
né hlýða

VIÐ FLJÓT OG STRÖND

I

Þegar fljótaguðir verða ástfangnir
þá er eins gott að leggja á flótta

Þetta vissi hin skynsama Arethusa
úr fylgdarliði Artemisar

Náði í heila höfn
á eyjunni Ortygíu

Kastaði mæðinni
breytti sér í uppsprettu
létti stórum og spratt
jafnharðan upp

í stöðugum
glitrandi létti

Rann til sjávar
sameinaðist

Will not shout nor be silent
Nor obedient

The power of writing
The only power that I submit to

Have never wanted to shout or be silent
or obedient

BY RIVER AND OCEAN

I

When river deities fall in love
it's time to take to your heels

She knew this wise Arethusa
votary of Artemis

Took final refuge
on the island of Ortygia

Caught her breath
changed into a spring
and thus unburdened surges
up immediately

in ceaseless
glittering translucence

Flowed out to sea
became one

útrunnu vatni
fljótaguðsins

II

Bjartur vindstrekkingur
gárar hafflötinn
úti fyrir Sýrakúsu

gárar hugann
þar sem Æskýlos
vinur minn
brosir úr fjarska

Vindur og haf
hvorki gamalt né ungt

Eilífð leiklistar
með grímu
vinds og hafs

grímu sem hugsar
til Æskýlosar
brosandi í fjarska

III

Höfnin
siglingaráformin
órar tímans
Tipasa

Stytta af frjósemisgyðju
bakvið gler á safninu
föst í sínu keramikformi

126

with the spent waters
of the river deity

II

A bright strong blast
ripples the face of the sea
just off Syracuse

ripples the mind
where Aeschylus
my friend
smiles from afar

Wind and ocean
neither old nor young

Eternal drama
with mask
of wind and ocean

A mask that thinks
of Aeschylus
smiling in the distance

III

The harbour
the urge to sail
the delirium of history
Tipaza

The statue of a fertility goddess
behind glass in the museum
trapped in its clay form

Hreyfingarlaus
frjósemisgyðja
í eilífri kyrrstöðu

Úti fyrir agave
öðru nafni þyrnililja
einnig kölluð eyðimerkurlilja

Árum saman
býr hún sig undir lífið
Springur loks út
sannkölluð sprenging lífsins
hverfula stund

Siglingaráformin
frjósemisgyðjan
órar tímans
Tipasa

IV

Olía á eld
Olía á tregans eld

Gluggarnir dyrnar
gjörvallt húsið er hljóðfæri
blásturshljóðfæri

fyrir heyrnarlausan vindinn
sjónlausan hafnargarðinn
hamslaust brimið

Olía á eld
Olía á tregans eld

Motionless
fertility goddess
in eternal stillness

Outside is the agave
sometimes known as the thorned lily
or the desert lily

For years on end
it prepares itself
then blossoms finally
a true explosion of life
a fleeting moment

The urge to sail
the fertility goddess
the delirium of history
Tipaza

IV

Oil on fire
oil on burning blues

The windows the doors
the entire house is an instrument
a wind instrument

for the deaf wind
the sightless wharf
the wild surf

Oil on fire
Oil on burning blues

Vissara að gæta sín
á gerviefnum
arineldurinn gæti sloppið laus
í gervisilkisloppinn

Hreint silki hins vegar
það kviknar ekki í því
sviðnar bara
og lyktar eins og mannshár

Olía á eld
olía á tregans eld

v

Blómin fljóta
í helgum straumi
fljóta í draumi

Blóm og eldur
kom í ljós
í Haridwar

Sviflétt vatn
hraðskreitt
léttara en grámóðuvatn
Jökulsár á Fjöllum

Sviflétt vatn
kom í ljós
í Haridwar

sveif heilagt
til sjávar

Safer to be on one's guard
against synthetic materials
a spark from the fireplace might catch
the imitation silk robe

Pure silk on the other hand
does not catch fire
it simply melts
and smells like singed hair

Oil on fire
oil on burning blues

    v

Flowers float
in the sacred stream
float in a dream

Flowers and fires
come to light
in Haridwar

Light dappled water
rapidly flowing
lighter than grey cloudy water
of Jökulsá á Fjöllum

Light dappled water
came to light
in Haridwar

glided sacredly
to sea.

fúr
LJÓÐORKULIND
(2012)

TILKYNNING FRÁ HEIMSÞINGI DEMANTANNA

Nú getum við ekki meir
getum ekki sýnt
þessa ítrustu hörku lengur
þessa gljáandi hörku

Einu sinni vorum við kol
tók árþúsundir árþúsunda
að ná fram
demantahörku okkar

Nú getum við ekki meir

Í morgun var ákveðið
á heimsþingi okkar
demantanna
að við skyldum linast
já við yrðum að linast

Þetta eru mótmæli okkar
gegn ójöfnuði mannanna
gegn óréttlæti mannanna

Vér demantar heimsins
höngum alltaf á sama fólkinu
í hálsmenum hringjum
eyrnalokkum höfuðdjásnum

Nú ætlum við að linast
Það er niðurstaða þessa þings okkar

from
POEM ENERGY SOURCE
(2012)

ANNOUNCEMENT FROM THE INTERNATIONAL ASSEMBLY
OF DIAMONDS

Now we cannot do any more
can no longer show
this extreme hardness
this glowing hardness

We were once coal
it took thousands and thousands of years
to bring out
our diamond hardness

Now we cannot do any more

In the morning it was decided
at the international assembly
of diamonds
that we will soften
yes, that we would soften

That is our protest
against the inequality of man
against the injustices of man

We, the diamonds of the world
always adorn the same people
in necklaces, rings,
earrings and tiaras

Now we are going to soften
that is the conclusion of our assembly

Ætlum að linast
jafnvel þótt það verði til þess
að við lekum úr höfuðdjásnum
niður í hárið á drottningum
eins og gamalt sæði
úr löngu dauðum hermönnum

Jafnvel þótt það verði til þess
að við lekum
niður úr hálsfestunum
eins og berklaslummur
úr liðnum líkum
efnilegra ungskálda

Lekum úr hringjum og eyrnalokkum
eins og kóleruríkar hrákaslummur
á gangstétt í þriðjaheimslandi
svo fólki skrikar fótur
í fínustu hverfum heimsborganna

Skrikar fótur í okkur
sem ákváðum í morgun

á heimsþingi okkar
demantanna

að linast

We are going to soften
even though it leads to us
leaking out of those tiaras
down through the hair of queens
like old semen
from the bodies of long dead soldiers

Even though it leads
to us leaking
down from necklaces
like consumptive phlegm
from dead bodies
of promising young poets

Leaking out of rings and earrings
like choleric spit
on the pavement in a third world country
so that people miss their footing
in the finest areas of town

Miss their footing in us
who decided this morning

at the international assembly
of diamonds

to soften

Sigurður Pálsson poet, novelist, playwright and translator, was born in 1948 at Skinnastadur, Iceland. He has worked as a professor at the University of Iceland and the National Academy of Dramatic Art, and as a cinema producer. Since 1975, Pálsson has published fifteen books of poetry, and has been nominated for many prizes – in 1993 for the Nordic Council Prize for Literature, in 1995 and 2001 for the Icelandic Literary Prize, and again for the Icelandic Literary Prize in 2008, this time winning with *Minnisbók* [Memoranda]. His poetry has been translated into more than twenty languages, with selections of his work being published in French in 1993, Bulgarian in 2005, Italian in 2006, in Spanish in 2008, in Bengali and Hindi in 2009 and in Arabic and again in Italian in 2013. In November 2013, a new and more comprehensive selection of his poems was published in French.

As well as poetry, Pálsson has written three novels a first book of memoirs, and eleven plays for the theatre, all of which have been staged, his most recent play, *Utan gátta* [Off Target], winning him the ITP Playwright of the year in 2008. He has also written an opera libretto, *The Moonlight Island*, which received its world premiere in Beijing in 1997, and a second book of memoirs, *Bernskubók* [Book of Childhood] which was published to huge critical acclaim in 2011.

Pálsson is a highly-regarded translator, having translated twenty-seven titles (poetry, plays and novels) from French into Icelandic, including works by Camus, Genet, Adamov, Arrabal, Ghelderode, Feydeau, Bailly, Carrère, Queffélec, Prévert, Éluard, Augé, Deforges, Châtelet, Vinaver, Anne, Kvaran, Schmitt and Cordelier, and two plays by Arthur Miller.

Recipient of numerous literary awards in his native Iceland, Pálsson was made a Chevalier de l'Ordre des Arts et des Lettres by the French Minister of Culture, Jack Lang, in 1990, and a Chevalier de l'Ordre National du Mérite in 2007 by the President of France.

MARTIN S. REGAL was born in London in 1951. Educated in the UK and the USA, he is now a member of the Faculty of Foreign Languages at the University of Iceland, but has also taught at Kunnliga Tekniska Högskolan and the University of Stockholm. In addition to teaching and translating, Regal has also been the drama and dance critic for *Morgunblaðið* and, briefly, a film critic for the Icelandic National Broadcasting Company (RÚV). His book-length works include a monograph on Harold Pinter and temporality, *Harold Pinter: A Question of Timing* (Macmillan, 1995). He is currently preparing the first edition of Harold Pinter's plays to appear in Icelandic as well as completing a critical work, *Tragedy*, for Routledge's 'New Critical Idiom' series.

Among his many translations are *The Saga of Gísli Sursson* (2003) and *The Saga of the Sworn Brothers* (in *Comic Tales and Sagas from Iceland*, 2013), both for Penguin Books.

Published poetry by Sigurður Pálsson:

Ljóð vega salt (1975)
Ljúð vega menn (1980)
Ljóð vega gerð (1982)
Ljóð námu land (1985)
Ljóð námu menn (1988)
Ljóð námu völd (1990)
Ljóðlínudans (1993)
Ljóðlínuskip (1995)
Ljóðlínuspil (1997)
Ljóðtímaskyn (1999)
Ljóðtímaleit (2001)
Ljóðtímavagn (2003)
Ljóðorkusvið (2006)
Ljóðorkuþörf (2009)
Ljóðorkulind (2012)

Poetry Collections:
Ljóðvegasafn contains *Ljóð vega salt*,
Ljóð vega menn and *Ljóð vega gerð* (1996)
Ljóðnámusafn contains *Ljóð námu land*, *Ljóð námu menn*
and *Ljóð námu völd* (2008)
Ljóðlínusafn contains *Ljóðlínudans*, *Ljóðlínuskip* and
Ljóðlínuspil (2010)
Ljóðtímasafn contains *Ljóðtímaskyn*, *Ljóðtímaleit* and
Ljóðtímavagn (2013)

Illustrated Books with Poems:
(illustrations by Bernard Alligand)
Jardin (2006)
Accordéon (2007)
Îles et presqu'îles (2009)
Le troisième livre (2011)
Le rituel des sens (2012)

Translations of Poetry into Icelandic:
Prévert, Jacques, *Paroles* (1987)
Éluard, Paul, *L'Amour la Poésie*
and other works (1995)

ARC PUBLICATIONS
publishes translated poetry in bilingual editions
in the following series:

ARC TRANSLATIONS
Series Editor Jean Boase-Beier

'VISIBLE POETS'
Series Editor Jean Boase-Beier

ARC CLASSICS:
NEW TRANSLATIONS OF GREAT POETS OF THE PAST
Series Editor Jean Boase-Beier

ARC ANTHOLOGIES IN TRANSLATION
Series Editor Jean Boase-Beier

NEW VOICES FROM EUROPE & BEYOND
(anthologies)
Series Editor Alexandra Büchler

details of which can be found on the
Arc Publications website at
www.arcpublications.co.uk